Praise for *Talking About Retirement*

"What a very dull subject 'retirement planning' used to be for most people! But now, with so many changes to pensions' law, tax law and the pension benefits offered by employers, the need for retirement planning has never been greater. Despite my own career in financial services, Lin Ashurst has long been my own trusted personal adviser and I have first hand experience of her extraordinary knack for bringing these matters to life by combining the practical with her deep knowledge of the subject and her thorough analysis. The timing is certainly right for this book. For the reader, it should be an invaluable guide to a more fulfilling, and a less uncertain, long term future."
Sir Mervyn Pedelty, Retired CEO of The Co-operative Bank and Co-operative Insurance Society

"Because of Lin's advice, I'm pretty sure that at the age of eighty I'll have sufficient income to be able to fly to the Seychelles, buy a Harley Davidson, learn the tenor sax and open a dive shop. And I'll still have enough left for the occasional tequila. Read this book, and join me there in a few years' time."
Tony Robinson, Actor and Writer

"Lin Ashurst is one of the few people I know who takes real pleasure in understanding the complexities of the UK's pension and tax laws. This enthusiasm even manages to engage those of us who tend to blank out at the mere mention of VAT or CGT."
Vanessa Branson, CEO and Hotelier

"Feeling confident about retirement isn't just about making sure the money won't run out – it's about feeling excited about life after work, having the confidence to take on new challenges and opportunities. Most of us have many more years of healthy life after formal retirement than our parents and grandparents had; for many of us it can be one of the most enjoyable times of our lives. Thanks to Lin and her team I'm not only financially prepared for retirement, I'm really looking forward to it."
Baroness Murphy

"Lin Ashurst writes clearly on a complex subject and comes over as if she really cares. That is what you want in an adviser."
Lawrence Lever, Chairman, Citywire Financial Publishers

"My work as a pension lawyer has convinced me that our pensions' system is both hopelessly over-complicated and highly unlikely to provide financial security for us in retirement, let alone fulfilment. But it has been Lin's inspirational advice that has revealed the way forward for me and many others. She has an exceptional ability to cut through the complexity, combining her financial acumen with a deep insight into .... as people."
.... ;almon

Talking About Retirement

The secrets of successful retirement planning

LIN ASHURST

KOGAN
PAGE

Publisher's note
Every possible effort has been made to ensure that the information contained in this book is accurate at the time of going to press, and the publishers and authors cannot accept responsibility for any errors or omissions, however caused. No responsibility for loss or damage occasioned to any person acting, or refraining from action, as a result of the material in this publication can be accepted by the editor, the publisher or any of the authors.

First published in Great Britain by Kogan Page Limited in 2009

Kogan Page Limited
120 Pentonville Road
London N1 9JN
United Kingdom
www.koganpage.com

© Paradigm Norton Financial Planning Ltd, 2009

ISBN 978 0 7494 5515 6

British Library Cataloguing in Publication Data

A CIP record for this book is available from the British Library.

Typeset by Jean Cussons Typesetting, Diss, Norfolk
Printed and bound in India by Replika Press Pvt Ltd

Contents

Foreword

Lin Ashurst bounced into my life 20 years ago with all the energy of a wagtail on Pro Plus. She was enthusiastic, lively, interesting and funny, characteristics I don't usually associate with financial planning. Her methods were unusual too. I wanted her to look after my money and sort out a pension for me, but she kept asking me questions about my life, my hobbies, my dreams and my passions. I hope she'll forgive me saying so, but initially I was a little cynical. It all sounded a bit 'alternative', and I'd cast my kaftan and beads aside a decade previously. But slowly I grew to realize that behind these questions a shrewd business brain was at work. She wanted to help me generate enough money to ensure I could do what I wanted during my retirement, rather than dedicating my life to making money and having no strategy whatsoever for using it to enhance the rest of my life.

Since that first meeting, Lin has remained my financial planner, and though the current economic squalls look set to blow pretty hard for the next few years, I'm confident that in my old age I'll be protected because of the sound financial plan she and I have put together.

I've learnt a lot from her, particularly that we all need to change our thinking about what to do when we stop working full-time. The National Insurance scheme, to which so many of us have dutifully contributed for so long, won't provide us with the secure pension we thought it would. Nor are our independent and business pension plans likely to shower us with the largesse we once dreamt of, as interest rates stay low and more and more old people make demands on the accumulated pension funds.

So will we have to work for longer than we anticipated? Will we have to raid the savings we'd hoped to leave to our grandchildren, or will we be forced to reduce our standard of living to make sure there's enough money left to keep us going to a ripe old age? Not necessarily. We are confronted by tough challenges, but they can be overcome if we are clear sighted and put in place sensible strategies.

Because of Lin's advice I'm pretty sure that at the age of 80 I'll have sufficient income to be able to fly to the Seychelles, buy a Harley Davidson, learn the tenor sax and open a dive shop. And I'll still have enough left for the occasional tequila. Read this book, and join me there in a few years' time.

Tony Robinson (Actor and Writer)

Introduction

'I've been retired for 22 years and it's been the best part of my life.'
Ernest Dennis, interviewee for *Talking About Retirement*

Like everyone else, I've read the thought-provoking statistics on the extent of the ageing population. But what the statistics don't tell us is what it's like to be approaching retirement, or to be going through the early stages of this life-changing event. From working with clients of all ages, and from talking to a lot of people, I know that the subject of retirement exercises many minds. People want to make their retirement matter to them but they don't want somebody else's vision of the ideal retirement to be forced upon them. During our childhood and youth we have to conform to social norms – attending school and university. During our working lives our behaviour is conditioned by the need to earn a living and raise a family. But in retirement we can eventually kick over the traces and live life just for us.

For me, probably the most powerful statistic is this one from Dr Ken Dychtwald, special adviser on global ageing to HSBC: 'Two-thirds of all those who have made it to the age of 65 in the history of mankind are today walking the earth.' Says it all, really.

THE YOUNGER OLD

The shift in distribution of the population towards older people will continue, at least for the next 50 years. This shift has led to the coining of a new term for those people aged 65 to 84: the younger old.

The younger old have attitude. A recent international survey carried out by HSBC, *The Future of Retirement: What the World Wants*, confirmed that an increasing number of people want to do something new when they retire. Many of them have a positive view of retirement. They do not see retirement as a time purely for rest and relaxation. They are anxious to build on their optimistic views to ensure an active and fulfilling retirement. This attitude will become an increasing trend as the baby boomers start to retire.

The baby boomers, those people born between 1946 and 1964, started to hit 60 in 2006 and are a wall of people who've changed the way society works in each of the life stages they've moved through. The baby boomers are not prepared to compromise; they live life on their terms. They will change the way we live in retirement.

WHO AM I?

My name is Lin Ashurst. I am a financial planner and I work with clients advising them on retirement planning and life planning. Life planning is helping clients use their assets to achieve their desired lifestyle.

I am a baby boomer and am giving retirement more than a passing glance. As much as anything, this book is about my own personal search for what I need to do to make my retirement a success.

WHAT IS RETIREMENT?

Retirement is a comparatively modern concept and the perception of it has changed over the years. Initially retirement was viewed as a period of rest between work and death. Then it came to be seen as a reward for a long working life, in other words a slightly longer period of rest between work and dying. Finally it has come to be seen as a period of leisure. Going forward it will be seen as an opportunity to do new and exciting things, things that you can only dream about doing when you are working.

I asked the people I spoke to when writing this book for their definition of retirement and here are some of the answers:

- 'When you are not working for cash full-time.'
- 'Doing something different.'
- 'Achieving financial independence.'

- 'Being in a position where we choose what we want to do without it including earning a lot of money.'
- 'I think there is a difference between retirement and getting old.'

RETIREMENT AND GETTING OLD ARE DIFFERENT

Retirement and getting old used to be the same thing. When the average period spent in retirement was only a few years, as it was several decades ago, then retirement was synonymous with old age. But now that retirement can last for 40 years there is a period of time between stopping work and getting old. In advanced economies retirement is seen as something that should precede the onset of old age.

DO WE NEED A NEW WORD FOR RETIREMENT?

Someone I spoke to said: 'I think you need to find a snappy word for being able to do what you want to do when you want to do it.' Should we find a new word for that period of our lives between stopping work and getting old? After all, the word 'retire' means to withdraw and that's the last thing that modern retirement is about. But I hate euphemisms; we all know what we mean by retirement and changing it and calling it something else in the hope that it will be more palatable to those thinking about doing it is futile. Instead of changing the word, let's try to change people's attitude to retirement so that they view it as a life-enhancing time when they have the freedom and ability to do all those things they couldn't do when they were working.

THE BASIS OF THE BOOK

During my work with clients I have been keen to know how people deal with the issues and challenges that face them as they approach and progress through retirement. And over the years I've been intrigued why some people make their retirement happy and fulfilling while others find it a less positive time. I've become convinced that the successful retirees have a formula for cracking the code for a happy retirement. This book reveals the results of my exploration and analysis of that code, what I call 'The Retirement Code'.

THE STRUCTURE OF THE BOOK

The book focuses on what came out of talking to people; their own experiences of retirement. But because pensions, investing and financial planning are such an integral part of making a success of retirement, there are chapters on these subjects too, which readers can dip in and out of as their fancy and 'need to know' take them.

Each chapter heading includes a quote from someone I interviewed for the book. I could have used famous people's quotes but why should I when the interviewees gave me such profound and inspirational material?

THE PEOPLE I TALKED TO FOR THE BOOK

I interviewed 31 people for the book. I appreciate that this doesn't constitute a scientific survey but it has shed light on how real people are dealing with their retirement planning, and has helped me report precisely the issues facing people approaching and in retirement.

The people I interviewed are comparatively well off but very few of them started out that way. Almost without exception they have all worked and planned hard to make provision for their retirement.

At the end of this introduction is a list of the people I interviewed, with very brief details of their situation together with a quote that captures their view of retirement. It is a *dramatis personae*. I have not used the interviewees' actual names but everything else about them is real.

The ages of those interviewed range from 47 to 84, some are married, some single, some divorced, some are widows and widowers. I split the interviewees into three groups. The first group I term pre-retirees, people who are some way off retirement but nonetheless thinking about it. The second group, transitional retirees, are just on the verge of, or in the early stages of, retirement. The third group are the post-retirees who have been retired for two years or more. Age isn't the factor that determines which group someone is in. For example, one interviewee is age 51 but has been retired for over two years so is a post-retiree, while another is age 68 but has only recently retired so is classed as a transitional retiree.

A word on ages: I really dislike it when newspapers refer to someone's age – you know the sort of thing, 'So and so, father of two, aged 56'. Quite often the fact that he is 56, or the father of two, has absolutely no bearing on the story that is being reported. However, I do use ages in the book because I think it is important to see where people sit on the age spectrum, as it often helps to explain their attitude and approach to retirement issues.

THE QUESTIONS I ASKED

At the end of this section I've included a list of the questions I asked the interviewees. Asking yourself the same questions may be a good starting point for helping you formulate your own retirement plans.

READ THE IN-DEPTH STORIES

The full stories of the transitional and post-retirees' journey into and through retirement are available on www.paradigmnorton.co.uk. I hope the book makes you want to read more about the individuals who have given me such a perceptive insight into what it is to be retired.

RETIREMENT ISN'T JUST EXERCISING OUR BRAINS, IT'S EXERCISING THE GOVERNMENT'S BRAIN TOO

In October 2006 the government launched a 5-year initiative to look at all the dimensions of ageing, from biological to social and cultural aspects. Professor Alan Walker, director of the New Dynamics of Ageing Programme (NDA), said: 'All of those who will be aged 80 and 90 in 30 years' time are alive now and that means that, if adjustments can be made in their ageing process, both their future prospects and those of British society can be transformed.'

The stark truth is that the government cannot afford to meet the maintenance and care costs of an ageing population and is all too well aware of the funding issues it is facing, hence the NDA initiative. Its best bet is to keep people healthy longer and working longer so that they will be less of a drain on the country's resources. And quite frankly that is our best bet too.

LET'S NOT START BY BEING NEGATIVE

One of the people I interviewed for my book was Sarah Joyce. Sarah cared for her mother who was 106 when she died. This is what she said:

I think that one of the benefits of having my mother to live with me was that she was a remarkable woman. Everybody's got a sense of assuming you get to a certain age and everything drops off. But there was nothing wrong with her. I think that she was one end of the standard and I feel privileged to have been part of that. It's very sad, obviously, when you don't meet that standard and very few of us will – but at least it's there. And, for example, we shouldn't always say things like 'When my eyesight's gone.' She could still read the telephone directory without glasses (remember she was 106!). You don't have to say this rots, or that rots. It doesn't necessarily, and I think we shouldn't be so negative about old age.

I want to show you how fulfilling and exciting retirement can be and potentially how long it can last. To show you that if you make financial provision for retirement you stand a much better chance of enjoying it and living a retirement life on your terms, not on State-benefit terms. And, ultimately, if you've made financial provision, a much better chance of cushioning yourself against some of the downsides of getting old, such as the cost of long-term care.

I also want to show you that a successful retirement doesn't just depend on making financial provision, it also depends on making emotional and practical provision.

But, most of all, I want to show you that retirement has the potential to be the best time of your life.

DRAMATIS PERSONAE

The following is a list of the people I interviewed for the book together with brief details. Further details are revealed in the book.

Pre-retirees

Nell Priest
Age 51. Single.

> *'The assumption in society now is that when you retire – if you are fit and healthy – you will have some alternative career or commitment, but actually making that transition into a fulfilling retirement seems to be a very hard thing to do.'*

Nell is a partner in a legal practice in London.

Mary Edwards
Age 59. Married to Gerald.
Second marriage for both. No children.

> 'The idea of having more time to myself, more time to myself where I can just sit and not always be on parade. That's how I think about retirement.'

Mary has been Chair of several Health Authorities and worked closely with the Mental Health Act Commission. She has a special interest in health and social care of the elderly and sits on several government bodies.

Gerald is a mathematician.

Brad and Julie Isles
Ages 60 and 50. Second marriage for both.
Each has two children to previous partners and they have one child together.

> 'It horrifies me! The thought of 'being retired'. Doing something different is what I call it.'

Julie Isles

Brad and Julie are involved in advertising businesses. Julie runs her own company and Brad is a partner in a medium-sized organization.

Carl and Maggie Armstrong
Both age 52. Married with two children.
Maggie is Ernest and Diane Dennis's daughter. Ernest and Diane Dennis were also interviewed for the book.

> 'I'm concerned that once I stop working my reason for living will go, so I want to have something in retirement that replaces that, and it has to be something that's constructive.'

Maggie Armstrong

Carl and Maggie run their own architectural practice.

By his own admission Carl has a tendency to be introspective and refers to himself as 'Mr Misery', a term he coined to describe his sometimes bleak but often deep view of life – and death.

Gary and Gloria Knight
Ages 48 and 47.
Married with three children, one of whom is disabled.

> *'It doesn't surprise me that some people say they work harder in retirement once they've given up salaried work, because it's not the personal commitment to work that bothers me, it's the fact that I've got to be in this office from 8 o'clock until 6 o'clock every Monday to Friday and I've got that commuting at the end of it.'*
>
> Gary Knight

Gary works as head of operations at a large company in the city and Gloria is a nurse.

Transitional retirees

Richard and Samantha Jeffries
Ages 68 and 66. Married with two children.
Sean Jeffries' older brother. Sean Jeffries was also interviewed for the book.

> *'We haven't stopped being the people we were. You don't, in retirement, do you? If you were motivated before you retired, you'll be motivated after you retire.'*
>
> Richard Jeffries

Richard is an eminent medical specialist who recently stood down from his job as head of a research organization.

Samantha is a puppet maker and puppeteer. She uses her puppet-making skills for the illustrations for the children's books she writes.

Deirdre Goode
Age 57. Widowed. Two children.

> *'I have enormous freedom and I have enormous independence to do what I want to do. I never have to consult anyone about what I am going to do and I like that.'*

Deirdre was a solicitor but left her job when her first child, Ingrid, was born and never returned to paid employment.

Sean Jeffries
Age 58. Married to Jean. No children.
Richard Jeffries' younger brother. Richard Jeffries was also interviewed for the book.

> *'What do I like best about retirement? We previously lived a very regulated life. I would leave home at 20 past 7 in the morning and I was seldom home before 8 o'clock in the evening. So there was little free time and anything important that we wanted to do needed planning in advance. Now we can be much more spontaneous.'*

Sean sold his marketing business in 2004 and now does occasional consultancy work.

Greg Eaton
Age 64. Widower. Two children.
Vicky Alder
Age 60. Divorced. Two children. Greg's partner.

> *'I think we older people have the right attitude – we don't feel old. I'm 65 in three weeks' time. I don't feel my age, I don't think anyone feels their age these days. And all the powers I had when I was younger, I've still got those. And I'm still physically very fit.'*

Greg Eaton

Business owner and entrepreneur, Greg has retired twice!

For most of her working life Vicky was employed in the family business – haulage and sand and gravel.

Michelle Stansfield
Age 58. Widow. One child.

> *'I now do things because I want to, not because other people want me to. I think the really good thing about retirement is that suddenly you're just doing it for yourself and that's a real big plus.'*

Recently retired from a senior executive position as head of banking operations at a well-known financial institution.

Post-retirees

Amy Pillinger
Age 71. Divorced. Three children.
Colin Matthews
Age 71. Widower. Three children. Amy's partner

> 'Retirement? It's wonderful! I thought it was going to be good but it's even better than I imagined.'
>
> Colin Matthews

Amy was a teacher but when her first child was born she gave up her job to concentrate on bringing up her family.

Colin worked as a chemist for a large industrial organization.

James and Denise Dent
Both age 63. Married with two children.

> 'It doesn't matter how many people tell you that they are busy all the time in retirement, you don't really understand what they do until you retire yourself. And we are retired and, in that sense, it's the nicer times now, but we're still busy people.'
>
> James Dent

James worked for an international company as one of their top executives.

Denise's job has been to look after James and to make a home for them wherever they were living.

Wanda Purcell
Age 74. Twice widowed. Two children.

> 'There's a whole lot of good things about retirement but the best of all is that I can please myself and I don't need to feel burdened by duties.'

As a young woman Wanda worked as a journalist and, after that, was very actively involved in politics.

Sam and Joan Jarvis
Ages 67 and 69. Married (second marriage for Sam).
No children.

> *'When people ask me what I do in retirement, I say I'm doing all the things I've been waiting to do for the last 35 years.'*
>
> Joan Jarvis

Sam and Joan both worked for the BBC. Sam produced natural history programmes and Joan was a designer.

Ernest and Diane Dennis
Ages 84 and 76. Married. Two children.
Maggie Armstrong's parents. Maggie Armstrong was also interviewed for the book.

> *'When you are working and you're about to retire there are these unknowns – the challenges are there. But now, from our point of view, we've made a success of retirement and we look back and think: actually, it's even better than we thought it would be.'*
>
> Ernest Dennis

Originally from South Africa, Ernest and Diane moved to London where Ernest worked in the city dealing in mining investments. They have been retired for over 20 years.

Belinda Crompton
Age 62. Divorced. Two sons.

> *'I do find it immensely exciting just seeing what life brings every day. I don't think I felt this level of excitement even as a small child.'*

Since she retired Belinda has owned and run a small farm and wood in Dorset.

Maddy Lister
Age 73. Widowed. Four children.

> *'My life was quite constrained before I retired and I feel that I've been terribly lucky – I've been able to do things in retirement which I've wanted to do, which I couldn't do before. I've certainly enjoyed my retirement – as far as I've got at the moment!'*

Maddy retired when she was 60. Her partner, Rupert, was an author and since his death she has managed his literary estate.

William and Helen Kennett
Ages 79 and 56. Second marriage for both.
William has one child to his first marriage and Helen has two.

'I said to my doctor the other day, "This new drug that you might be putting me on, I've been told it only works for five years" and he said to me "You're 78. What do you want me to say? In five years' time you'll be 83. Have you got plans?" I said, "I've got plans way beyond 83, doctor." '

William Kennett

Until he retired William Kennett was a very successful store manager, setting up and running flagship stores both in the UK and overseas.
Helen was also a store manager.

Sarah Joyce
Age 68. Widowed. Three children, one of whom has mild learning difficulties.

'It's the freedom. It's the opportunity to do things perhaps you've not done before that you would like to have done, and it's the sense of self-fulfilment that you have lived your life fairly worthily.'

Sarah's husband, Donald, worked for an international organization. Consequently the family spent a lot of time abroad and Sarah's job was to look after them.

Barry and Anita Rudd
Ages 51 and 49. Married. No children.

'I want to be like my father. When he died the church was overflowing – I didn't know he knew so many people. In many ways he'd lived a boring life – he got married, worked hard, retired – and yet there was something important about it. It did strike me as a life worth living.'

Anita Rudd

Before he retired Barry was managing director of a FTSE 100 company.
Anita has reached the top of her profession in computer technology and is considering a gradual retirement over the next two years.

THE QUESTIONS I ASKED

When I was interviewing people for the book I wanted to encourage them to explore their feelings about retirement and to find out how prepared they were for this life-changing event.

The following are the questions I asked. Going through the questions and answering them yourself should give you some clue as to how ready you are to cope with the challenges retirement poses and the opportunities it offers.

Retirement planning – exploring retirement opportunities

1. What plans have you made for the transitional period into retirement? What opportunities and/or problems do you think you might encounter?
2. What financial and practical plans, if any, are you making for your retirement? If none, do you plan to do so in the future and what are they likely to be?
3. What excites you about retirement?
4. What fears and concerns do you have about retirement?
5. What ambitions do you want to fulfil in retirement?
6. What, if any, specific goals will you set yourself in retirement?
7. What do you see as the biggest advantage of being retired?
8. What do you see as your greatest challenges in retirement?
9. How important will it be to you where and how you live in retirement?
10. How will you motivate yourself in retirement?
11. How will you keep mentally active?
12. How will you keep physically active?
13. How will you safeguard your health?
14. Have you ever encountered ageism? If so, when and how did you deal with it?
15. How has your appetite for risk, in all areas of your life, changed as you've got older? How do you see this change continuing in retirement?
16. How will you provide for yourself financially in retirement?
17. How will you provide for yourself spiritually in retirement?
18. How do you currently give, in terms of time and other non-financial resources, to your family, your local community, wider society and the world? How do you see this developing/changing in retirement?

19. What losses, in the broadest sense of the word, do you see yourself having to cope with in retirement?
20. What do you see as the benefits and challenges of partnership and friendship relationships in retirement and how do you plan to deal with them?
21. What plans will you make for the later period in retirement when you may be less able to look after yourself?
22. How do you think you will live your life differently in retirement?
23. What would need to have happened in your retirement for you to consider it a success?
24. Do you have a particular retiree role model? If so, who and why? What could you learn from them?

1

Hopes and best bits

'I was lying in bed this morning and thought in 13 years' time I shall be 70 and that's actually quite interesting because I still feel very young. I think we've been extremely fortunate because we missed the war and everything's gone our way. We've been a very lucky generation.'

Deirdre Goode

Forget the statistics, they don't tell you how real people feel about retirement; they don't tell you what those approaching retirement are looking forward to and what those in retirement are enjoying. Neither do they tell you how to make a success of your retirement.

The purpose of this book is to help everyone make their retirement the best it can be. I started by asking people how they feel about retirement; exploring what people are looking forward to most and what those who are already retired are enjoying the most. Are they the same? Does life in retirement live up to expectations?

In this chapter I make no attempt to come up with solutions or recommendations; that comes later. This is an opportunity to report the real retirement issues people face and to let them set the agenda for the rest of this book.

It is also an opportunity to get to know the people I talked to.

DREAMS AND REALITY

Looking forward to having more time

Almost without exception, those approaching retirement, the pre-retirees, talked about looking forward to having more time. Carl

Armstrong was typical: 'The time freedom is something that you would anticipate being a bonus. Time is the one thing that I just don't have – and being able to fill it up with what I want to do.' Carl is 52 and he and his wife, Maggie, also 52, run a busy professional practice. They have two children who are both at university.

Carl and Maggie have little time to think about what retirement might look like to them. As Carl says: 'We just don't physically have enough time and we can't create enough time to explore it. We know that retirement could be good, it should be a huge vista that opens up, but we are still in the valley of work at the moment.'

I liked Carl's expression 'the valley of work' because it implied that retirement was on the peak, in the sunshine, something to aspire to.

Nell Priest, 51, is a solicitor working in London. At the moment she can only dream about losing the time constraints her job imposes on her. Shortly before I interviewed her she had been chatting to one of her previous colleagues who had just retired: 'He said the best thing for him was to get up in the morning and stand in the shower and not think: I have to be out of here in five minutes because I've got to get the 8.25 into town. And he said that that was real luxury.'

Post-retirees on having more time

Are post-retirees enjoying having more time? Absolutely – James Dent is 63 and has been retired for several years and his answer is typical: 'It's the expanded time to do things. It's that feeling that yes, we're busy, but we're not having to fit things into half the time you'd really like to do them in.'

By her own admission Joan Jarvis is not a lady who lunches. When the design work she was doing came to an end in her early 50s, the thought of spending the rest of her life without a purpose horrified her. She tried charity work but that didn't fulfil her. Then she decided to attend a course in textiles. She loved it and became extremely proficient. She now takes commissions and organizes exhibitions of her own and others' work. She travels the world exploring the tradition of textiles in other countries and brings back her findings to incorporate into her own work.

At the age of 69 she agrees that retirement gave her the time and the freedom to pursue a passionate interest. She has no trouble answering when people ask her what she is doing with her time: 'I say I'm doing all the things I've been waiting to do for the last 35 years.'

Looking forward to doing what you want to do

Combined with having more time pre-retirees are most looking forward to being able to do what they want to do. Gloria Knight, at 47 the youngest of the interviewees, is still in the middle of juggling work, family and home life: 'I think it's the ability to do what you want. To go where you want. To do whatever you want to. That's the way I look at it. Maybe that's simplistic and not realistic. I don't know, but that's my thought of retirement.'

Post-retirees on enjoying doing what they want to do

When he worked, James Dent operated at a hectic pace. As one of the senior executives of an international company he was used to working long hours and travelling widely. When asked what she was enjoying most about being retired, Denise, his wife, half-jokingly said: 'I now know that James is going to turn up on holidays.' She went on to tell me stories of the many times they had booked holidays but because of work commitments they had had to cut them short. 'We had a holiday going from Boston to Toronto to New York and he never arrived!' James protested, 'I did arrive in New York for the house hunting. I got there for two days' house hunting instead of ten days' holiday.' Now life is no longer dominated by work, 'We can please ourselves. We're not constricted by office routines or business trips and commitments like that', says Denise.

Sometimes doing what you want to do in retirement includes continuing to work but preferably on your terms. Barry Rudd reached financial independence before the age of 50. His future is financially secure and he no longer needs to work to earn money. Now age 51 he is doing something he is passionate about: helping a young and developing company grow and become successful. He is paid one-fiftieth of what he was paid before he retired: 'I have gone through the phase of what excited me when I was 35, earning a large salary, and I have achieved that. Now I don't see why there would be anything that would excite me more than being able to do what I want, when I want and it not really mattering whether I earn a lot or not a lot.'

Barry was the first interviewee to talk about the advantage of not having a label in retirement in the same way you do when you are working: 'When you're working what you think of somebody depends on the job they do. It's a typical question: "What do you do?" And you might say "I'm a marketing manager for whatever" and they put you in a box and they've got you greyed up. And so when people ask me what I do now they can't work out whether I'm good or bad.'

Looking forward to not having to do what other people want you to do

All the interviewees were either looking forward to or enjoying being able to do what they want to do but several of them also mentioned the flip side: not having to do what other people want you to do!

But when I explored this, I found that this ability came with age rather than with retirement; as people grow older they care less what people think of them, which gives them the confidence to say 'no' if they don't want to do something.

Gloria, my youngest interviewee, who is some way off retirement: 'I don't care what people think about me any more. There's half a dozen people in this world whose opinion I care about. Anybody else, if they don't like me, I don't care just so long as I don't hurt the people I love.'

This put me in mind of something I once heard: 'At 20 you care what people think about you, at 40 you don't care what people think about you and at 60 you realize that they've never been thinking about you at all.'

Post-retirees on not having to do what other people want you to do

Amy Pillinger, who is 71, summed it up rather well when she was talking about the benefits of growing older coupled with retirement: 'To a certain extent you can choose what you want to do and I think you can be a bit more forceful and say "No, I am not going to do that" whereas when you were younger you were probably a bit more conformist.'

Looking forward to an expanding social circle

At the moment Nell Priest works long hours and has little time for socializing, other than with her work colleagues. She explained why she thought retirement would help her increase her social circle: 'I think one benefit of being retired is that you're in a more relaxed environment where you can meet some more like-minded people and that way you can expand your circle of friends.'

Post-retirees on expanding social circles

Fifteen years ago, at the ages of 69 and 61, Ernest and Diane Dennis moved across the country to live near their daughter. They had lived in their previous home for over 14 years and had a big circle of friends there. According to Diane, expanding their social circle when they moved wasn't a problem, quite the reverse: 'When we came down here we certainly made many more friends. We've got more friends now than we've ever had and fitting them in takes time!'

The time freedom that comes with retirement doesn't just enable people to form new friendships, it often enables them to rekindle old ones; friendships that might have been difficult to maintain during a busy working life are revived.

Looking forward to being selfish – in a positive way!

Michelle Stansfield is what I term a transitional retiree, someone who is very close to, or in the early stages of, retirement. Until she retired eight months ago she held a top executive position in one of the UK's leading financial institutions. As a woman juggling career and family she knows what it's like to put others first. Since her retirement she has had an opportunity to think about what she wants out of life:

> I now do things because I want to, not because other people want me to. Of course, for a woman who works you've got a situation where you feel loyal to the job, then you look after your family and your husband and everything else, and you come at the tail end somewhere of all that. So I think the really good thing about retirement is that suddenly you're just doing it for yourself and that's a real big plus.

Michelle is enjoying what she refers to as her 'me time'.

Post-retirees on being selfish

It was the single post-retirees who talked about the advantages of being able to be selfish. Indeed, it was one of the consolations of being alone in older age. Wanda Purcell, a widow, is 74 and has led a very active life in journalism and politics. She confessed to enjoying being able to be selfish in retirement: 'It's a thoroughly selfish life. I have my little routines – when I do what I want to do – and I love it.'

Looking forward to losing the shackles of salaried employment

Pre- and transitional retirees saw retirement as an opportunity to lose things as well as an opportunity to gain things. When I asked them what they were looking forward to most, I should have been prepared for the answer: 'Not having to go to work!' After eight months of retirement Michelle Stansfield was still passionate about this: 'It's not having to go to work. I think it's different if you've never worked, or worked part time, but I think when you've been in the situation I've been in where work absolutely filled your life and everything else that happens, happens round the edges of the job – when you retire you suddenly find yourself with your life back.'

Gary Knight, Gloria's husband, is 48. While he holds a very senior position in the organization he works for, he is a salaried employee with the attendant constraints that imposes. Gary sometimes feels these constraints: 'It doesn't surprise me that some people say they work harder in retirement once they've given up salaried work. It's not the personal commitment to work that bothers me, it's the fact that I've got to be in this office from 8 until 6 every Monday to Friday and I've got that commuting at the end of it.' He is certainly looking forward to the day when he can find himself with his life back.

Post-retirees on losing the shackles of salaried employment

Do post-retirees still appreciate having thrown off the shackles of salaried employment? Colin Matthews does. Colin is Amy Pillinger's partner; he's 71 and has been retired for over 10 years. When I asked him what he enjoyed most about being retired he didn't hesitate: 'Not having to go out to paid work every morning, especially when it's snowing, that still gives me a kick – two fingers to my former employer.'

Looking forward to losing the responsibility of running a business

It was interesting that while employees were looking forward to losing the constraints their employment placed on them, the self-employed were looking forward to losing the responsibility of running a business and looking after other people.

Like many employers, Carl and Maggie Armstrong are operating in an increasingly regulated and litigious environment and are finding this challenging. They are aware that, because they are joint partners in their professional practice, it is difficult for them to mitigate any liability problems by placing assets out of reach of potential creditors. This does not worry Maggie. She feels that the ethical way in which they operate, combined with a robust professional liability insurance policy, will protect them. Carl is less sanguine about the situation. He says: 'I'm probably, I think, looking forward to the loss of professional liability. With what we do we are exposed with our professional liability and passing that on to someone else would be a worry gone.'

Post-retirees on losing the responsibility of running a business

Technically Sean Jeffries isn't a post-retiree because he is still in the process of retiring. However, I thought it was appropriate to use his comment on losing the responsibility of running a business in the post-retirees' section because he gave up running his business in 2004. In 1989 Sean took a big gamble – he bought the small marketing company he had been working for. The gamble paid off and in 2004 he sold his share of the firm to his younger partners. The move was the right one for him: 'The best thing is the absence of things, the absence of having the responsibility of running the business. I don't miss any of that. The cut and thrust was fine while it lasted but I'm glad it's gone, heartily glad.'

Greg Eaton, 64, is a born entrepreneur. He has always had an eye for good business opportunities and has built up several concerns from scratch. In 2004 he sold his shares in a business he had owned and run for 10 years and did something that everyone who knew Greg said he would never do – he retired! He has no regrets: 'I think that the thing that excites me most is that I don't have, any more, to think about getting out, going and looking after people, employing people, and everything associated with it – it's just something I don't have to do any more.'

Looking forward to losing the day-to-day responsibility of caring for children

Gloria and Gary Knight have three children: two girls and a boy, all in their teens. Their son, Thomas, is disabled and has learning difficulties. They are hopeful that with support Thomas will be able to lead an independent life when he reaches his 20s. Gloria is looking forward to retirement and sees it as a time for her and Gary: 'By the time we've retired the children will be settled and it's time for us. And I haven't got to worry about their problems. I know that's rubbish because you always worry about their problems but to a certain extent it's time for us to look after us, and go where we want to go and do what we want to do.'

Post-retirees on losing the day-to-day responsibility of caring for children

Is Gloria being too optimistic about retirement and life after the children are independent? Not according to Amy Pillinger; her children left home many years ago and are now in their 30s and 40s. She does still worry about them but is enjoying being free of that day-to-day responsibility of caring for them: 'I think this time, retirement, it's the best bit for me as a person. I'm not saying it wasn't good when I was a "mum", but the bit that's me is liking this bit best.'

Also post-retirees on having an opportunity to spend more time with children – and grandchildren

There is another side to this coin for those who are able to retire early. Helen Kennett, 56, is married to William who is 23 years older. It is a second marriage for both of them. When William retired 19 years ago Helen decided to give up work too. She says: 'I think the greatest advantage initially was being able to spend a lot more time with the children. In the years I worked I found balancing the job, running the home and looking after the children extremely hard work. I was always worried. I was always on the run. So to suddenly have the wonderful advantage of always being here for them was brilliant.'

If grandchildren are the reward we get for not killing our children then many of the post-retirees are enjoying their rewards.

Both Denise and James Dent's grandparents died before they were born and they feel that they missed out on an important relationship; they don't want their own grandchildren to miss out on that relationship. But when James was so busy working and they were moving around the world it wasn't always easy to spend time with their sons. This was further complicated because one of their sons had married a French woman and was living in France and the children were being brought up French speaking. Neither Denise nor James spoke French well. So Denise made one of her retirement goals 'To make friends with my grandchildren'. Since James retired they have had the time to pursue this goal. They have made a concentrated effort to improve their French and spend more time with their grandchildren. They now feel they are well on their way to making great friends with their grandchildren.

Looking forward to getting fitter

Mary Edwards is one of the pre-retirees who are looking forward to having more time for exercise. At the moment she is finding it hard to accommodate a keep-fit regime into her working life: 'I do nothing during the week, no time. At the weekends we do a walk, three miles or so, any more than that and we're both on the floor!'

Post-retirees on being fitter in retirement

Whether it's the fact that they have more time, can take advantage of off-peak gym membership rates or realize that retirement is more enjoyable if you are physically able, many post-retirees claim they are fitter in retirement than they were when they were working. Belinda Crompton is walking much further than three miles: 'I do long-distance walking. It's really great and I didn't start that until I retired but I've done some fantastic walks.'

ANTICIPATIONS ONLY MENTIONED BY THE PRE-RETIREES

Looking forward to not being on parade the whole time

During our working lives there is a certain requirement for us not only to behave in a certain way but also for us to dress in a certain way. This applies regardless of the job we do; there seems to be an acceptable 'uniform' for all occupations. For Mary Edwards, 59, the requirement is onerous because she spends a lot of time in the public eye. Mary works within the health service as a clinical academic, specializing in mental health and ageing-related issues and has served on several public bodies. She is well known in government circles as well as in medical circles.

As a public figure Mary sometimes feels the burden of being on show the whole time: 'You are on parade a bit, you know, and if you're opening something, and I do quite a bit of opening things, you've got to keep smiling! Otherwise you know a photograph will appear of you in some local paper with you looking miserable, so you've really just got to keep looking cheerful.' She went on to say: 'You do have to get dressed up, it's so nice to come home to trousers.' Mary is looking forward to having more of the trousers and less of the dressing up when she retires.

Interestingly, none of the post-retirees mentioned the benefit of not having to 'dress for the job'; they've probably got used to being able to wear exactly what they want.

ANTICIPATIONS ONLY MENTIONED BY THOSE EXCITABLE TRANSITIONAL RETIREES

I found that transitional retirees were discovering a whole cornucopia of 'best bits' about being retired. They were like children let loose in a sweet shop. They mentioned advantages of being retired that neither the pre- nor post-retirees mentioned and seemed to be discovering a new excitement every day.

Being spontaneous

As Michelle Stansfield says: 'You know, when you work you just cannot do things on the spur of the moment. Everything has to be planned. Everything has to be organized and whilst I still do that to a certain extent, I couldn't manage without the diary, it's really nice to get up in the morning and think "Right, what shall I do today?" as opposed to "Right, I've got these 35 things to fit in today." '

Sean Jeffries has retired gradually over the past two years. Since he sold his stake in the marketing company he set up he has been working as a consultant on a freelance basis, working with clients he likes and he feels he can add value to. In this way he has been able to control his workload, rather than the other way around. His excitement at being retired and having more time is palpable: 'We previously lived a very regulated life. Now we can say, right, the sun's out, we'll dig out the map and say, look, there's so much of England we've never experienced, let's go off and do this or do that.'

It's almost like 'Five Go On Retirement'!

Being irresponsible

Brad Isles is aged 60. He is just about to sell his share of a business that he has spent 30 years building and he then plans to retire. Brad made me chuckle when he answered my question about what he was looking forward to: 'When you asked me what will be the biggest advantage of being retired, I thought: I can be irresponsible now.'

The delight in being irresponsible or 'naughty', as one interviewee termed it, was something only transitional retirees mentioned. Richard and Samantha Jeffries, ages 68 and 66, describe themselves as having a strong work ethic. Richard has been at the head of his profession for many years; a respected authority on complex medical conditions on which he still lectures and writes books and papers. Last year he stood down as head of the research organization he has worked for since the late 1990s. Samantha is a successful author and continues to write and be published on a very regular basis. Richard admits: 'I think both of us grew up feeling that you had to do things properly, and do your best, and so I think the idea of being slightly naughty is new. We'd never been to the cinema in the afternoon before, we occasionally do now and we feel naughty.'

However, transitional retirees didn't always find it easy to adjust to having more time and Richard was one of them. He had been used to getting up at 5.00am when he worked and admits: 'I'm having to learn to lie in bed!'

FULFILMENTS ONLY MENTIONED BY THE POST-RETIREES

Swapping the indoors for the outdoors

I was surprised at how many post-retirees said that one of the biggest advantages of being retired was having the opportunity to spend more time outdoors. Office technology not only keeps us office bound, it often keeps us desk bound too. James Dent was passionate about the outdoors: 'Retirement was a chance to be outside more. When I worked, outside was something I looked at through windows. I'd been brought up a country lad and couldn't wait to be outside again, whether it's in the garden, golfing or walking, I just want to be outside and not inside looking out.'

FINAL THOUGHTS ON HOPES AND BEST BITS

I have left two comments for the end of this chapter; one from Carl Armstrong, a deep-thinking pre-retiree, and one from Ernest Dennis, a post-retiree.

Time to prepare to meet your maker

Carl Armstrong self-titled himself 'Mr Misery' because he felt that others might view his often deep and thoughtful comments as negative. I found some of Carl's comments, such as the following one, quite profound:

> Once you are in retirement it emphasizes the fact that life is a one-way journey. I think that the death aspect (being such a wonderful misery) is one of the things that I see as an upside of retirement. You do have time, if you wish, to look at your demise within the context of mankind or anything else. It didn't occur to me until the other day that we are actually all stardust. You are only just passing through in this form and it's one of the things in retirement that hopefully you should be reflecting on.

Being stress free

I will leave the last comment on advantages to Ernest Dennis. Ernest was born in South Africa in the early 1920s and came to England in the 1970s where he worked in a demanding job in the City. He retired in his early 60s. Looking back on that time he reminded me that our working lives are subject to many pressures, not just the pressure of our jobs, and that retirement often corresponds with being released from several of those pressures: 'Before I retired it wasn't just the stress of the job, it was continually stressful. There was the stress of commuting, getting the children through school and university, repaying the mortgage – this, that and the other. But when you retire all that is removed, and I don't have that stress any more – it's a beautiful life.'

2

Fears and realities

'A challenge is not to become a typical retired person. I consider myself to be rock 'n' roll generation and I always want to live a comparative rock 'n' roll lifestyle.'

Brad Isles

If it's a beautiful life, what are people worried about? Well, it appears that the answer to that question is – lots!

So what are the downsides? What worries do people have about retirement and are their worries justified? Let's look at the fears and concerns those approaching retirement have. And from those already retired, let's discover what really are the biggest challenges of retirement.

Concerns and fears depend on where you are on the retirement spectrum. Those who have not yet retired are worried about how they will achieve fulfilment, job satisfaction in retirement if you like. Those who have retired are more concerned about how they will cope with losses: health, partner, home and independence.

All fears and concerns benefit from being recognized, planned for and managed. I have not dismissed pre-retirees' fears as unfounded simply because post-retirees do not currently have an issue with a particular concern. Usually the post-retirees don't have an issue with the concern because they have taken pre-emptive action.

The fear of running out of money before you die

Everyone, pre-, transitional and post-retirees alike, shared one concern: having enough money to fund the kind of retirement life they wanted to live.

Brad Isles was certainly not alone when he said: 'I suppose running out of money is my number one fear. Having to cut back and do without things that we've been used to enjoying.' Brad went on to say: 'I know if you have health problems that are hopeless then money cannot save you, but running out of money is a bigger worry to me than health.'

Julie, Brad's wife, agrees: 'I worry about money – about not having enough. There are things I need and things I want to do. I don't think we have an extravagant lifestyle but we seem to spend a fortune.'

Brad is about to retire and lose the salary he has been receiving each month for the past 40 years. Several post-retirees mentioned how frightened they felt when their earnings, and their earning capacity, dwindled and finally ceased and they were reliant on pension and other unearned income.

Post-retirees on the fear of running out of money before you die

None of us know how long the financial provision we have made for retirement will need to last. As Amy Pillinger says: 'It's cash versus longevity.' Amy's mother was 93 when she died and her father was 89: 'Genetically I am programmed to live to a ripe old age. But you don't know, nobody knows how long what you've got has to last you. And you're thinking should I do this or that now, but then maybe if you got to 81 and you were still lively you'd think "Oh, I wish I'd still got that to look forward to and I've done it – and spent the money." '

The fear of not filling your time constructively

Many pre- and transitional retirees were worried about this particular issue. Maggie Armstrong: 'One of the things I fear is not filling my time constructively and it just being a playground time. I think there must be a point and an aim to life and, at the moment, that's filled by a job.'

There is a great deal of social pressure these days to 'have it all'. In the workplace this has meant juggling a host of demands on our time. Are we in danger of this attitude spilling over into retirement? Will people feel under-achievers in retirement? Are Maggie and Carl victims of this pressure? Isn't retirement all about less pressure, not more?

Post-retiree Wanda Purcell says that she sometimes feels that people expect you to have a very full and active retirement and if you are not out learning three new languages, going to tai chi classes and walking the Pennine Way you're letting the side down. She thinks it is important not to feel guilty: 'One of the advantages of retirement should be not feeling guilty about *not* doing things.'

Unlike her husband, Barry, Anita Rudd has not yet retired. She has a senior role in the IT department of a major retailer. At the age of 49 she is planning to retire in the next year or two. She makes the excellent point that you are only an under-achiever in retirement if you don't achieve a target you've set yourself: 'I know from past experience that I am quite good at just drifting through the day and time goes by very pleasantly. If you're not worried about achieving something then it doesn't matter if that has happened to you. But if you are not achieving something you want to achieve then you should worry about it.' One big difference between work and retirement is that you, not your employer, partners or shareholders, set the targets!

Post-retirees on the fear of not filling your time constructively

None of the post-retirees mentioned that they had a problem filling their time constructively, in fact quite the reverse.

Belinda Crompton, age 62, thought she had a happy marriage. She and her husband, Derek, were planning their retirement in Dorset and Belinda had moved to the farm they'd bought there while Derek continued to work in London during the week. Then Derek met someone else and eventually divorced Belinda. At the time she was devastated but on reflection she realizes that it was the best thing that could have happened to her: 'In a way divorce is like retirement because it is the process of giving up that enables you to find the new part of yourself, the part that was not being used before. To rebuild your life, using the same bricks as it were, to form a completely different shape.'

After the divorce Belinda kept the farm and the wood that was attached to it. Now she is busy working the wood and has set up a healing centre in the farm grounds. Not having enough time to do all she wants to do is more of a problem for Belinda: 'At the moment I am really, really concentrating on trying to slow it down a little bit because it is too tempting to just keep taking things on. I do need time off too and one of the biggest problems with retirement is that you don't get weekends. It's a seven-day-a-week job. It's only too easy to allow yourself no time to do things simply for pleasure, the things that you might have done when you worked.' It hadn't struck me until

Belinda mentioned it that retirement is a full-time job – you don't get weekends off!

James Dent says: 'Like all retirees it's finding the time to do everything! People at work find it extraordinary but have you ever heard anybody retired say anything else other than: "I don't know how I had time to work, I really don't!"?'

The fear of not having any new challenges in retirement

While Anita Rudd admitted that she could 'drift' through life very happily she did add: 'But I just feel somehow that I would want to take a look back at the week and say "I've done that this week, or I achieved that" or whatever.'

Carl Armstrong agrees; he believes that it is important to keep challenging yourself in retirement: 'I would want to do things to challenge who I am, not necessarily just for enjoyment but to discover something new.'

Nell Priest had admitted that not only was she looking forward to having more time in retirement, she was also looking forward to using it constructively: 'I guess retirement is an opportunity to break out of the rut and to see whether there are new challenges that can be met and enjoyed.'

Post-retirees on the fear of not having any new challenges in retirement

Like most people in retirement Belinda Crompton has had no problem finding and rising to new challenges. Since retiring she has made a commitment to managing the farm and the wood on an ecological basis: 'I suppose the thing that I was most keen on when retiring was to find something that offered me a new challenge, something I hadn't done before. I started retirement by doing two degrees: ecology and conservation. Since then I've spent time putting what I've learnt into practice.'

The fear of not taking advantage of the opportunities that retirement offers

Most people approaching retirement are, as Brad Isles said, looking forward to being irresponsible. But for Gary and Gloria Knight there is no guarantee that this will ever happen. Their disabled son, Thomas, may never be able to live an independent life. Gary is not a fit man and suffers from two chronic illnesses. He was very aware of the implications of his situation when he told me: 'My only concern is that, for whatever reason, I am not able to take advantage of the opportunities that retirement offers.'

Their work and family commitments have not allowed Gary and Gloria to develop interests that they might pursue in retirement: 'Neither of us are hobbyists. We don't have some passion that's in the background that we're suddenly going to explore but that doesn't mean that we can't find things that we enjoy.'

Post-retirees on the fear of not taking advantage of the opportunities that retirement offers

Life does not necessarily run smoothly at any time; some of us may have few obstacles in the way of achieving a fulfilling retirement, others have many. The challenge is to learn to cope with whatever life throws at you.

It was Sarah Joyce who said: 'I think when we talk about retirement everybody hopes that you're going to have financial security, you'll have good health, you'll have good friends, you'll have opportunities to do things you've perhaps not done before. Well, we don't all have everything we want at any point in life.' Ten years ago Sarah's husband, Donald, was murdered in a random killing the day before he retired. Now, at the age of 68, she has learnt to come to terms with her situation. She has a daughter, Heather, who has learning difficulties. Heather lives independently but needs emotional, financial and practical assistance from Sarah. In addition, Sarah's mother, aged 106, lived with her until she died recently. She believes that it is not easy to identify all challenges in advance: 'Challenges, you don't know. And whatever they are you have to meet them. They are not challenges I set myself but I can see that challenges might be imposed upon me and I just hope that I'll deal with them in whatever way I can.'

The fear of becoming irrelevant

Nell Priest has watched with interest how those people who have retired from her practice have fared: 'Quite a few of the more senior people I've seen retire in the past, principally men I have to say, were programmed from the time they started work to think that they would reach the top of the tree and then they'd stay there and be successful. They don't ever see anything beyond the day that they retire from the organization and I think they equate retirement with failure in that regard.'

People are so often defined by what they do, and not who they are, that the fear of losing that definition is very real. As Carl Armstrong says: 'I don't want to become irrelevant. However much good or harm I have done, I think that as a professional I am always relevant to someone because I am giving them advice and to lose that would be a fear of retirement.'

Post-retirees on the fear of becoming irrelevant

Several post-retirees admitted that they did have a problem when they lost their work status and faced the challenge of letting go and moving on.

As Joan Jarvis put it: 'You feel you're on the scrap heap, even though you're not, but you feel you are because people have moved on, they've employed someone younger. It's not an easy time.'

It was Sam Jarvis who spoke about the sadness of what he called 'the bar-proper-uppers', people from his organization who had retired but who would come back, prop up the bar and tell everyone that they were still worth employing and was there any work for them. Sam was determined that this was not going to happen to him, but he had to be realistic about what would happen when he retired:

> I had to realize that most of the people I dealt with in my working life would fall away like autumn leaves once I left; people I was very friendly with, doing business with, and they had no allegiance, once I had no deals to talk through, no budgets to talk through, they would vanish – and they all have. So you have to realize well before this stage comes that it is likely to happen. I did realize it but it must come as a great shock to a lot of people who don't.

The fear of being in ill health and losing fitness

While the pre- and transitional retirees didn't mention a fear of ill health as much as the post-retirees mentioned it as a challenge, it was certainly a concern, especially if the interviewee had had a close experience of ill health or, as in the case of Mary Edwards, worked in the geriatric section of the medical profession.

Mary Edwards's work has given her a valuable insight into the problems associated with ageing:

Remember I've spent my entire life working with older people and although you know the statistics and you know it's unlikely that you'll get dementia, and you know that it's unlikely that you will get physically ill until quite a short time before you die, I do have a horror of becoming chronically ill, and seriously in pain or demented. That's the major thing, I think, because once that happens it constrains everything you do and then you really are in trouble.

It was Mary who pointed out that physical exercise has been proven to be most effective at delaying the onset of many illnesses, including dementia, but she admits that keeping fit is a challenge: 'I think keeping fit is a challenge. Getting half an hour's exercise every day is probably the one thing that will do more for you than anything else, and that's been something that I've been very bad at all my life.'

Samantha Jeffries is a transitional retiree. She has just nursed a friend through a serious illness: 'What worries me most is the physical deterioration, and mental too. It's what happens to your body and your mind that you can do very little about. And it's how you deal with that when it happens. I think that's the biggest thing I have to face.'

Post-retirees on the fear of being in ill health and losing fitness

Post-retirees have seen more ill health, disability and death among their peer group than the pre- and transitional retirees have; it is inevitable, therefore, that the post-retirees recognize that maintaining health is probably their major challenge.

'I think the fear is probably the ailing, the dwindling of mind and body and I end up a cabbage in a home' – Joan Jarvis expressing a concern shared by virtually all post-retirees.

And Ernest Dennis, aged 84, very fit but fully aware of the challenge: 'The greatest challenge for me is staying healthy. We've got the financial means to go into homes and that, so that's not going to worry us. Health's a very difficult thing to assess because you don't know what will happen to you. I don't really see anything else as a challenge, apart from staying healthy.'

Like most post-retirees, having identified the challenge of maintaining health, Ernest Dennis has devised an exercise and dietary regime that keeps him fit.

The fear of relationships turning sour

'Twice the husband on half the money', while sexist, is a good working definition of retirement for couples. During your working life you may spend relatively little time with your partner, probably a few hours in the evenings and at weekends. In retirement you could be spending all day, every day, in each other's company. This might put a strain on the relationship, at least initially, until each one of you has defined your new roles and space.

Gloria Knight is some way away from having to share the whole of her space with Gary but she is already concerned: 'It does worry me that Gary will be under my feet. It worries me a lot. I know what he's like. He gets bored. He's quite happy for a little while but then he starts to get twitchy, and I think this is something that's going to be ad-infinitum. So he needs to find something to do, so far he hasn't found it, but he needs to start looking.'

Post-retirees on the fear of relationships turning sour

Virtually everyone agreed – there is a period of adjustment when retirement takes place and couples spend more time together than they ever have before. All the post-retirees in relationships agreed that they had gone through this period of adjustment and often had several spats until things settled down.

Usually, after a period of adjustment, relationships do settle down and couples work out some ground rules for their retirement lives together. Generally the advantages of the companionship partnerships provide outweigh the disadvantages of having to redefine how you live.

But retirement is a reckoning time in relationships; weak marriages are vulnerable, strong marriages should, and do seem to, get stronger.

Joan Jarvis had watched her friends retire and knew that they had found it hard to adjust to sharing their space on a full-time basis: 'Some things are difficult for the woman, because your husband's around a lot more and perhaps he's not knowing what to do. It was an adjustment. But we got there.'

Not all couples 'get there'. William Kennett, Helen's husband, had been married for 38 years when he started to approach retirement. For some time he had felt that he and his wife had grown apart: 'What I didn't have at home was companionship. I realized that what I might be prepared to accept whilst I was working and only spending a few hours in the evening and at the weekends with my wife, I couldn't accept in retirement, knowing that we would be together all day and every day.'

Shortly before he retired William left his wife and subsequently married Helen. He admits that financially he is not as well off as he would have been if he had stayed married to his first wife but this is more than outweighed by the happy retirement life he has led: 'I don't have the wealth in hand, shillings and pence, I have the wealth in other things.'

The fear of being lonely

It was the single pre- and transitional retirees who were most concerned about being lonely in retirement.

Deirdre Goode, 57, gave up her job as a solicitor when her children were born. Her daughter, Ingrid, is now 24 and a solicitor in London. Her son, Tim, is 21 and has just finished university. Deirdre's husband died seven years ago and she misses him: 'One of the main fears is loneliness. Although I have a lot of friends I spend an awful lot of time on my own, particularly winter evenings. I've seen people get very old and be very, very lonely and I think as the years go on that increases.'

Post-retirees on the fear of being lonely

Post-retiree couples did not mention loneliness as a challenge, but couples will not stay as couples until they die; simultaneous deaths are rare. Divorce, separation, widowhood and widower-hood will mean that some of us will have to adjust to life on our own.

Maddy Lister, age 73, was widowed in her early 30s and brought up four children on her own. The partner she subsequently lived with died 10 years ago and she now lives alone and agrees about the winter evenings. She also highlights a problem facing many older people: how loss of physical capabilities can affect the quality of your retirement:

I don't mind being by myself provided I've got plenty to do but in the winter I get a bit low sometimes because I hate the winter. I hate the cold weather and I feel less inclined to go off somewhere and do something or see people. Also I'm deaf and that's a big barrier to joining a lot of organizations because I have a great problem hearing and it's quite hard to come to terms with it because I'm getting deafer as I get older.

The fear of losing social contact

Nell Priest pointed out that if you have worked long hours for many years the majority of your social circle may be your work colleagues. When you retire you are not only waving goodbye to your job but you could be waving goodbye to a large part of your social network: 'I think I will miss my work colleagues and the work environment and that's not the same as missing being valued for what you do. It's just missing the companionship. If you've worked with people for 20-odd years and then you leave, you're bound to miss them.'

The potential loss of social contact hadn't worried Michelle Stansfield when she retired a few months ago until she bumped into an acquaintance she hadn't seen for some time. The woman was in her early 60s and confessed to Michelle that she hadn't seen or spoken to anyone for well over a week: 'I think the comment this lady made to me about not seeing anybody sticks in my mind a lot and I thought to myself: this is awful; how can you go from day to day, at her age, and not talk to anybody?'

Post-retirees on the fear of losing social contact

Post-retirees who had been very interactive with work colleagues and associates all admitted that they did miss this social aspect when they retired.

Sam Jarvis again: 'I think the most difficult thing is the absence of people. Obviously when you're part of an organization and leading teams, having that daily contact with lots of interactions, then when that's no longer there you do miss it. I still miss it and I'm not sure what I've done about it because I'm not necessarily that social.'

The fear of losing the 'structure' of work and having nothing to replace it with

Two years ago Anita Rudd had a 12-month sabbatical from her job. Her time off gave her a taste of what retirement would be like and it was during this time that she realized that she would miss the structure her work gives her: 'It's quite frightening because suddenly the structure of your life has gone. I did find towards the end of my time off that I wanted to put some structure back so you can plan ahead what you are going to do.'

Post-retirees on the fear of losing the 'structure' of work and having nothing to replace it with

Many post-retirees reported that, however well they had planned, it took time to build a structure into their retirement lives that worked for them.

In spite of filling his days in retirement, Sam Jarvis, age 67, still misses the structure that work provided to his life. Sam and Joan Jarvis met when they were both working in the media, Joan in design and Sam in production. Sam rose to dizzy heights within the production team of the BBC. He retired nearly 10 years ago. An extreme sports enthusiast, he owns and flies a micro-light. He also treks in the Himalayas, regularly takes part in charitable bike rides, is a volunteer at a wildlife sanctuary, plays the organ and as an expert ornithologist lectures on dedicated cruise ships. But even Sam with his myriad interests and pursuits admitted: 'Freedom is a challenge as well as a benefit, you know, because you wake up in the morning and think aaahh, empty day, no one's asked me to do anything, so you just have to fill it.'

FEARS ONLY MENTIONED BY PRE- AND TRANSITIONAL RETIREES

The fear of becoming incompetent at your job

Transitional retiree Sean Jeffries has had time to formulate his retirement action plan: 'How do you keep yourself stretched in retirement to stop yourself becoming a pudding? I think that the answer, in my case, is a cocktail of things. A bit of work, plus doing something new that's mentally stimulating and just doing things that interest me.'

However, Maggie Armstrong warns against the winding-down approach to working in the professional arena by doing a 'bit of work':

> I'd like to work less and I hear of people working a four-day week and it would be great, so I'd like to ease off. But there comes a time when you probably become dangerous, you work too little to keep in touch and you really should give up. It is more litigious these days and there is so much new legislation coming out that you have to get on top of and you can't do that working part time.

It would appear that those working in the professions are disadvantaged. In many other jobs you can work on a very part-time basis without actually becoming dangerous because you don't have to keep up to date with legislative and regulatory changes in quite the same way.

The fear of something awful happening early in retirement and all your planning being in vain

Sean Jeffries' father-in-law had worked hard all his life and had made good provision and great plans for his retirement but benefited little from it: 'His lesson was that you can make the best plans in the world and if you don't live long enough to enjoy them, that's it. He only lived 18 months after retiring so that was, if you like, an object lesson to us – don't leave it too long before you retire.'

Post-retirees had moved on from the 'suppose something awful happens just after we've retired' because it hadn't. However, they were more aware of their mortality and much more inclined to live in the moment.

The fear of being bored

If your work is time consuming, but fulfilling, and you have had little time to develop other interests outside work, it is understandable that one of your fears would be that you might be bored in retirement. Mary Edwards believes that this is the number one concern of her husband, Gerald: 'Gerald has this fear, he's constantly worried that he might be bored. He's got this feeling that there might be a problem. Personally I can't see it but until you let go you don't know.'

The fear of world calamity

It was the pre-retirees who expressed concerns about the wider future, not just for themselves but also for mankind.

Carl Armstrong wearing his 'Mr Misery' hat:

One of the problems I fear is that with rapid climate change and population change all bets on traditional retirement are probably off anyway. I just don't see that some of the things will either be there to look at or you'll be able to get to them or that it will be safe to get to them. And just staying alive here might be the biggest challenge we are going to be faced with. Retirement may be just staying alive.

The fear of becoming a stereotypical retiree

I have included this because it gave me a valuable insight into one particular fear that transitional and pre-retirees had expressed – that of becoming a stereotypical retiree. In my experience, and the results of my investigations have confirmed this, there is no such thing as a stereotypical retiree but it is nonetheless a concern. Brad Isles probably expressed the fear best:

> This is probably a glib answer but not falling into the trap that lots of retirees fall into. I don't want to go on coach holidays. I consider myself to be rock 'n' roll generation and I always want to live a comparative rock 'n' roll lifestyle. A challenge is not to become a typical retired person. I go to work every day through a town and the average age of the population must be about 70 and even when I'm 70 I won't want to be part of that. I always want to be going on motor races, going sailing, playing the guitar, whatever.

His wife, Julie, agrees: 'We are both appalled at the idea of a cruise! That's one thing we will never, ever go on – even if it was to escape from a country with a civil war!'

The challenge of maintaining standards

I was interested to explore the proposition that being a success allowed you to fail. If you had been a success in your working life, did this empower you to take a real risk in your retirement and try new things, knowing that you might fail? Not according to Richard and Samantha Jeffries; they are anxious to maintain the same high standards in their work in retirement as they had pre-retirement.

As recognized leaders in their fields, both Richard and Samantha have embarked on new pursuits in this transitional phase of their retirement. Samantha is still writing books and Richard is still involved in the medical profession but in addition they are going to work together on a project making moving toys. When I interviewed them they had just got back from a week's course on making moving toys. Being second best in this new endeavour is not an option for them, as Richard told me: 'If I make something, or Samantha makes something it's got to be the best thing you can possibly make or anyone could possibly make. I'm not interested in do-it-yourself type things. Both of us come from backgrounds where you're either very, very, very good, or else probably it's not worth doing, it's a bunch of rubbish. We're not interested in amateurism.'

Richard summed it up: 'Well, I think the challenge for both of us would be how long can we go on being intellectually alert and producing things that are actually worthwhile.'

CHALLENGES ONLY MENTIONED BY POST-RETIREES

The challenge of coping with losses

Wanda Purcell has been widowed twice. After the death of her second husband she met a man who became her companion, but he died a few months ago, leaving a big gap in her life: 'Learning to be happy in my own company. And that's about widowhood, and is about subsequent losses. And the challenge of losses. The challenge of losing a close companion, a travelling companion; the person I did nice things with, fun things with. I think the challenge is, I don't know how to put it better than being content with my own company. I do get lonely.'

The challenge of not procrastinating – because you don't have deadlines in the same way you would if you were at work

Lack of externally imposed deadlines was the reason most post-retirees cited for their tendency to put off doing things more in retirement than they had done during their working life.

Greg Eaton was anything but a procrastinator when he was running his businesses but now he admits: 'I'm a great "putter-off". When there's loads of time I leave it and leave it and leave it and then – whap! I'm not "not doing anything" but, if there's a job to be done, I'll do anything but the actual job!'

His partner, Vicky Alder, says the same: 'At this point in my life, when I actually have more time than I ever have, I leave things longer.'

The challenge of coping on your own

A few years ago Sam Jarvis fell 20 feet off a cliff: 'Stupid, you know, I just walked off backwards. I was looking at a bird and stepped backwards.' Joan takes up the story: 'He just disappeared out of sight. I saw him hit the rock and go behind. I couldn't see any more so I, of course, was screaming and running for help.'

Miraculously, apart from a few bruises and a dislocated finger, Sam was fine. But it did make them think what life would be like if one of them were to die. As Joan says: 'Losing each other, I think that would probably be the biggest challenge of all.' Sam puts it even more succinctly: 'Well, if Joan died I'd top myself because I can't think of life without her, it's as simple as that.'

The challenge of moving house when you need to downsize

Moving house is recognized as one of the most traumatic events you can experience. Usually, at some stage in your retirement, it will be necessary to downsize your home and this can pose a problem, especially if you have lived there for many years. Also, it has to be the right move – you cannot afford to get it wrong at this stage of the game. Ernest and Diane Dennis are in the throes of thinking about moving and Diane explains how they are feeling: 'I think we've reached the stage where we've got to think about smaller accommodation. This house is getting too big for us. It's going to be a challenge because we've lived here for 15 years. Of course, moving house is always a challenge. And it's always traumatic too. So we've got to be very sure it's what we want.'

FINAL THOUGHTS ON FEARS AND REALITY

Life is fragile and unpredictable. Belinda Crompton, a post-retiree with a commitment to live in the moment, put it into perspective:

> I tend not to worry because what I have discovered in this period since I stopped work is that those things you worry about are not the things that happen and vice versa. Therefore I don't concern myself with what happens when I am no longer able to physically do all the things that I am doing now because I have absolutely no idea whether I will be able to continue to do this for another 20 years or another 10 days!

SUMMING UP

No two successful retirements look the same. What fulfilled one person's criteria for a happy retirement would ruin someone else's. Brad and Julie Isles dislike coach holidays and cruises, claiming that they wouldn't go on a cruise even to escape from a war-torn country! But going on cruises may be the very thing that contributes to making someone else's retirement a happy one.

All successful retirements might be different but they all have some common elements, some basic planning components that once identified, planned for, achieved and maintained help each and every retiree build their own successful retirement. This book aims to help with those basic planning components. It aims to help people achieve a happy and fulfilling retirement.

Read on...

So there we have our agenda. The idea of having more time, being able to please yourself, doing new things, making new friends excites people in a way it never did a generation or two ago because the time spent in retirement is longer, healthier and fitter than it has ever been. But people do have concerns about how they can make their retirement the best it can be. By talking to people about their hopes and fears I have been able to pinpoint specific issues that, if addressed, will help them achieve their best possible retirement. Having sought the wise counsel of those who have made the successful transition into retirement, coupled with my experience, knowledge and expertise, what follows in this book is a code for a successful retirement: The Retirement Code.

If you are interested in reading more about the people I interviewed for the book and their stories, don't forget to visit www.paradigmnorton.co.uk.

3

Looking good, feeling great

'How do I safeguard my health? By sensible eating and drinking.
Unfortunately I have no will power but that's the theory behind it!'
Colin Matthews

The English Longitudinal Study of Ageing (ELSA) is a study following a cohort of people born before 1952. Every two years members of the cohort are asked detailed questions about their lives. The plan is that over time we will build up a comprehensive picture of what it's like to grow old in this country. The study is in its infancy and only the results of three surveys (2002–03, 2004–05 and 2006–07) have been published to date, but already there have been some interesting findings.

ELSA's research has found that three-fifths of people aged 80 or over described their health as good, very good or excellent. This rather flies in the face of the image of decrepitude normally associated with the elderly.

But this finding doesn't mean that as we age we should take our health for granted. The three-fifths of people aged 80 or over reporting good health may well have worked hard to keep fit.

According to the statistics shown in the survey, each year more than 20,000 people in the UK develop angina for the first time and approximately 270,000 people have a heart attack. It is possible to reduce the chances of having heart disease or other life-threatening diseases by stopping smoking, improving your diet and taking more exercise.

So no more chip butties, fags or being a couch potato. Is all that abstinence worth it? It would appear that it is, because the survey reveals a wide diversity between the über fit and the not at all fit.

While our physical abilities decline as we get older, some of the oldest people in the survey maintained a high degree of physical ability. One example was grip strength in women, where the weakest women aged 52 to 59 fared worse than the strongest women aged 80 and over.

Several of the older interviewees for this book said that they felt physically fitter than they had at any time in their lives. Are they deluding themselves? Well, this is from the ELSA report:

> In spite of the overall pattern of decline with chronological age, the test results also show a great diversity of function, with some older people performing at higher levels than some of the middle-aged respondents. Similarly some of the youngest respondents have prematurely impaired functioning, showing the very different ages of onset of impairments: the link between chronological age and 'age-related' impairments is once again shown to be very loose.

It appears that it is not inevitable that as you age you become physically impaired and unable to do the things that you want to do. So working to preserve your health and strength for as long as possible could pay dividends.

I asked the interviewees what they did to keep fit: what they ate, what physical and mental exercise they took, whether they took supplements, whether they bought organic food, their views on private medical insurance and what regular health checks they had.

KEEPING PHYSICALLY ACTIVE

When we talked about keeping fit some of the interviewees, especially the pre-retirees, felt that they could do better. Even Mary Edwards, an expert on ageing-related issues and fully aware of the benefits of exercise, admits that she could do more: 'I was on a select committee on the science of ageing and we had wonderful expert advisers. I was really struck with the one thing that makes a difference to your life expectancy and your general fitness and ability to cope and that is the amount of exercise you get. To reap the benefits you only need half an hour of regular exercise each day, even if it's just walking.' And does Mary follow her own advice? 'I've been very bad at exercising all my life. I do need to do a bit more.'

Several of the pre-retirees said that they were looking forward to retirement so that they could get fitter; long hours spent commuting and in a sedentary occupation are not always conducive to maintaining fitness. Mary was one of the pre-retirees who recognized that retirement would give her more opportunities to get fit: 'I'm actually looking forward to having more time to do a bit more exercise and walking around a bit more. My current lifestyle doesn't let me do that. I'm always rushing around and I don't think that that's very good for me.'

And it seems to work! Post-retirees are taking advantage of that time freedom to get fit. And while some post-retirees admitted that they could do more, a greater number said that they were fitter in retirement than they had been during their working lives. Greg Eaton was one: 'I'm certainly stronger than when I first packed up work. I'm certain about that.' Greg still plays tennis, golf, goes skiing, swimming and does the garden: 'I get lethargic if I don't have exercise.'

According to the English Longitudinal Study of Ageing, if you have a medical condition the treatment you receive depends on what is wrong with you. If you've got something that the politicians are going to be questioned over the figures for, such as high blood pressure, heart disease or diabetes, then treatment is good. But for the less glamorous conditions of urinary incontinence, recurrent falls and poor balance, treatment is less satisfactory. Pity really, because although these afflictions are not big killers, they are miserable conditions and a bad fall in particular can signal the beginning of the end for an older person.

Keeping fit for as long as possible is undoubtedly helpful. Falls are often a result of muscle weakness, so exercising to maintain, and maybe even improve, muscle strength isn't such a bad idea.

And most post-retirees do realize that if they want to keep mobile they need to keep fit. Samantha Jeffries has made one of her retirement goals: 'To keep mobile. I mean both Richard and I have various decrepitudes! Joints and bones and bits that fall off and it's harder work now than it used to be so I want, as long as possible, to keep going physically so that we can do the other things that we want to do.'

Keeping fit for doing other things

It's obvious really – use it or lose it. It's possible to discover a whole new level of fitness in retirement. And the fitter you are the longer you will be able to go on doing things!

And the desire to go on doing things in retirement is a real motivation for keeping fit. People seem to find it easier to stick to an exercise routine if the aim of the exercise is to help them to continue doing something that they enjoy. Several interviewees who are pursuing physically demanding pastimes in retirement are working out so that they can continue to follow those pastimes for as long as possible.

Bearing in mind the amount of physical work Belinda Crompton carries out on her land, I had assumed that she didn't need a separate keep-fit regime. But like many retirees she has found that she needs to accommodate some form of disciplined exercise into her schedule so that she can keep on doing what she wants to do: 'My life generally is a large amount of physical labour, moving things from one place to another is what I seem to spend my life doing and it's usually heavy, but I'm getting stronger.'

To help prevent injuries which would curtail her work, Belinda does yoga: 'I find it absolutely fundamental for keeping stretched so that I don't damage myself by doing the huge amounts of physical work that I do. I go to a class once a week.'

Often a retirement pursuit or pastime calls for greater physical fitness and endurance than is required during your working life. For Richard Jeffries it was cabinet making that made him realize that he needed to get physically fitter:

> I only started going to the gym when I started doing a lot of cabinet making because it's physically hard work. I go very regularly, three times a week or so, because as you get older your joints and ligaments get a bit stiff. So now I'm quite strong and quite physically active. When you are doing cabinet making you're not lifting ton weights or anything but you need to be reasonably agile if you're going to work all day at it, lathing and fixing things. I hate going to the gym but I do it.

Exercise with a purpose is how Sean Jeffries describes his favourite keep-fit pursuit: 'I hate exercise regimes that involve someone shouting at you. I really can't stand that. I like doing jobs in the garden of a more violent nature: banging things, chopping things down, cleaning things out. There's a purpose to that!'

Gardening is another activity that post-retirees regard both as a form of exercise and as fulfilment. Vicky Alder has a large garden and helps her partner, Greg, with his garden. Vicky was speaking on behalf of several post-retirees when she said: 'Gardening's probably the most physical exercise that we do.'

Not everybody is playing golf!

There is a fair amount of golf being played. Michelle Stansfield is enjoying having time to play more golf and finds it physically challenging: 'Well, I have to say the golf is quite tough in the summer.'

But golf isn't everyone's keep-fit activity of choice. Sean Jeffries: 'I'm totally uncoordinated. Much as I like the idea of walking around the golf course, actually getting the bloody ball in the hole would be an impossibility. I think I would probably be banned from the golf course.'

And not everybody is exercising!

A few interviewees were thinking about exercising but weren't actually doing a great deal. Wanda Purcell wasn't even thinking about it: 'I've never done exercise. I don't believe in that. I don't walk anywhere. I take taxis. I walk into the village but that's only 200 yards to the nearest shop. I've never been for a walk as a walk in my life.' I have to say that Wanda is as fit as a fiddle but I suspect she is the exception that proves the rule.

Group sports

I was surprised at how many post-retirees, in spite of wonky knees, were playing group sports. However, it seems that this activity is more for the social benefits than the physical ones! Colin Matthews: 'I do play badminton once a week but it gets harder and harder. I feel it more and more on the following Saturday morning. But I like to try and keep it going if I can because it's also social, we've been playing together for more than 20 years.'

Maddy Lister is the same: 'I still play badminton although I've had various aches and pains over the last few months. I play with a group of ladies, all of us are in our 70s, but we also go to have a good laugh and a chat.'

Pre-retirement v post-retirement keep-fit routines

Although some post-retirees, like Richard Jeffries, are going to the gym, most are enjoying having the opportunity to get their exercise out of doors. The time freedom that retirement brings means that they can schedule exercise into the hours of daylight. Belinda Crompton: 'I like my physical activity to be outside. Physical activity inside, apart from yoga, just seems wrong somehow.'

On the other hand, pre-retirees talked about the time constraints in their lives that meant that their keep-fit regimes were either non-existent or very focused. And exercise often has to be fitted in around other commitments, resulting in working out on dark evenings or early mornings, which limits what you can do. Anita Rudd's time is in short supply and she needs a keep-fit activity that delivers quick results: 'When we first moved up here I thought we would go walking in the Lake District but, because I still work, weekends are precious so we don't. But the gym is handy and convenient so I do go and I'm fitter.' Anita has recognized that keeping fit is a lifelong pursuit but agrees that her activities may broaden when time allows: 'My aim is to keep fit into older life and that's why I initially got interested in going to the gym. I think I will also do wider things as I get older, perhaps do more walking.'

Although she works full time, pre-retiree Nell Priest has been able to fit her exercise regime into her day by, whenever possible, walking to and from meetings in London rather than taking a cab or the tube: 'It's amazing how far you can get in London if you walk from A to B. You can go an enormous distance in half an hour.' Nell intends to do more walking when she retires.

Seven years ago Brad Isles was diagnosed with angina. It made him review his lifestyle. He worked full time and had a long commute, often not getting home until 7.30 or 8.00 in the evening. It was difficult to fit exercise into his daily routine so he bought a dog: 'Both Julie and I enjoyed walking but we were a bit casual about it, having an animal that needs walking every day makes you more focused. Since we got the dog I've walked a lot. I'll walk the dog for 6–8 miles on a Saturday and again on the Sunday.' Several pre- and post-retirees get a lot of their exercise through dog walking. Dogs are a tie and can restrict your freedom to roam in retirement, but they do provide you with the motivation to exercise and, for many single post-retirees, with companionship.

Carl Armstrong (Mr Misery) continues to maintain the fitness regime he started as a teenager and sees himself continuing it for as long as he is able: 'In terms of running and things like that I've done it since teenage years and that's never stopped and I don't anticipate it stopping. It's funny though, it's never been easy, and you wonder why you do it, but if I don't exercise I'd just become grumpy and irritable.' – Really?

Taking advantage of off-peak fitness costs

As well as looking forward to doing more walking when she retires, Nell Priest is looking forward to being able to do more swimming: 'I'd like to join a swimming pool. Again it's another of those things on the list that I've never quite had time to really get into. And that's an advantage of retirement, of course, you're not competing with people at work for the time at the pool first thing in the morning.' Good point – being retired means that you can use exercise facilities during the day when it's quieter, and also take advantage of off-peak membership rates too.

When he retired Ernest Dennis's ambition wasn't a material one, it was to keep fit: 'The most precious thing in retirement is health and my ambition was to stay healthy, and physically active.' Ernest and his wife Diane keep fit by swimming. Off-peak membership of their local sports club enables Ernest to swim at a time to suit him; he's not bothered by early morning swimmers, he's more anxious to avoid the children who use the pool at the weekend: 'Every morning at half past seven I swim. We're members of the local gym that has a pool. I get up early in the morning and go and swim.' Diane joins Ernest on his early morning swim three mornings a week: 'We don't swim at the weekends because it's too expensive to be a full member.' In addition, Ernest plays bowls and he and Diane are keen walkers. When Ernest had his hip operation last year there was a brief break in their exercise routine but now they are back in full swing.

Holiday exercise

It was Maggie Armstrong who pointed out that when you are working very full-time, one way to incorporate exercise into your life is to go on exercise holidays. Maggie claims that that is the only sort of holiday that Carl, her husband, aka Mr Misery, will go on: 'I suggested activity holidays one day to Carl and he bought this book. He told me it was just what I was looking for but I think it was suggesting the equivalent of going up the north face of the Eiger.'

Carl disagrees: 'It's the steel roped walkways around the Dolomites, they were actually cut for moving the troops around in the First World War. They maintain them and it's not all crampons. Some of it's almost safe, just so long as there's no lightning because, obviously, if you are on the steel walkways when it's lightning then...' Mmmm – not sure I fancy that.

I'd always thought that cruises were the ultimate in lounging around doing nothing and losing fitness. But Joan Jarvis has a different view: 'On ships you're going up and down stairs all the time, up and down, up and down. Actually, I think one's fitter after one of those trips. I feel my muscles are quite well toned at the end of a cruise.'

Come dancing

One or two pre-retirees have become hooked on dancing classes as a way to keep fit following the celebrity dancing competitions on the television; Gloria Knight is one: 'I've done all sorts of dance lessons. I'm trying to get Gary to dance. Watch this space – maybe next year?' And Gary's take on this? 'I'll work until I'm 100 if it means I can avoid going dancing!'

Carers' time constraints

Those post-retirees who are looking after elderly parents or young grandchildren often find themselves in much the same situation they were in when they were working; not enough time in the day to pursue dedicated exercise regimes. Sarah Joyce, who cared for her mother who died recently at the age of 106: 'When I was looking after my mother it was finding time, it just wasn't available. It got swallowed up with other things.' But the sheer physical effort of being a carer is sometimes exercise in itself, as Helen Kennett, who helps to look after her grandson, points out: 'With my young grandson around I keep pretty active!'

When you can't pursue your chosen keep-fit activity

Until she had a problem with her knee Samantha Jeffries used to go to the gym and she loved it. Now she goes to a special Pilates class:

It's not like these very fashionable things with film stars in leotards, it's practical. It's more or less therapeutic Pilates and the teacher deals with people my age or a lot older, or younger people who have had injuries of various sorts. It's helped a lot. I slipped discs in my neck and I have this bad knee and was on quite strong painkillers and was thinking I was going to have to fold up and be an old lady, and this has made all the difference.

The cancer-fighting drugs that William Kennett takes mean that he cannot maintain the fitness regime he used to follow: 'Up to five years ago I used to do power walks. And when I say walk, I was going like a steam engine. But with the medication I'm on now I can't do that. I take seven tablets a day and on six of them it says one of the side effects is fatigue.' In spite of this he still exercises, but at a slower pace and for shorter distances. Helen, his wife: 'We still walk because it's nice walking along the prom, it's flat so it's easy for William.'

So if injury or illness prevents you from pursuing your usual fitness regime, see what else you can do, what else is out there.

The combined wisdom of keeping physically active

- Keeping fit is a lifelong pursuit. An advantage of retirement is that you have more time and therefore a greater opportunity to get fitter. And you can exercise out of doors when it's daylight and benefit from cheap, off-peak membership of clubs and swimming pools.
- Half an hour regular exercise each day improves your life expectancy, general fitness and ability to cope.
- The fitter you are the more you'll be able to do in retirement.
- Bad falls can signal the beginning of the end and are often the result of muscle weakness. Regular exercise can maintain and even improve muscle strength.
- If you feel that exercise has to have a purpose, align your fitness regime to complement, and perhaps improve, your ability to pursue a retirement occupation or pursuit. Or garden!
- Group sports can be socially satisfying as well as improving your physical fitness, knees allowing.
- You don't have to play golf, especially if you can't get 'the bloody ball in the hole!'
- Get a dog and walk it but remember it can restrict your freedom to roam in retirement.
- If you can no longer pursue your favourite exercise routine, look for an alternative.

REGULAR HEALTH CHECKS

Kicking your bad habits isn't the only thing you can do to stay healthy; getting a regular medical check-up can help too. When tested, 16 per cent of the women in the ELSA survey and 18 per cent of the men who had high blood pressure were not aware of the problem, presumably because they hadn't had a recent medical check-up. And yet, according to the report, there is strong evidence that, once diagnosed, treatment for high blood pressure is extremely beneficial, certainly up to the age of 80. And blood pressure is just one of the medical conditions that would benefit from early diagnosis and treatment.

Health checks while working – and beyond

Several of the post-retirees had had regular medical check-ups, paid for by their employers, when they were working. After retirement some continued to have regular check-ups. Greg Eaton: 'I still see the doctor I used to see every year in my old firm for a check-up. It's really thorough, he double-checks everything.'

Sean Jeffries thinks regular medical checks are important:

I'm a great believer in preventative medicine. And I'm a great believer in periodic health checks. It's something we used to do at my company, you'd go every year for a health check. Our local general practice isn't geared to carry out comprehensive checks and what we would hope to do is pay for more comprehensive checks; it doesn't cost much more than servicing your car. Thinking in terms like that, it's quite important.

James Dent, on the other hand, hasn't had a health check since he left work. Because he has good health he never thinks about it, although he did say that maybe he should review his stance on health checks: 'I think we are too casual about our health in any specific way. We don't have check-ups. I had all the check-ups when I worked because it came with the job but now I don't do it, I should do more.'

Like James, Wanda Purcell is blessed with good health: 'I'm awfully uninterested in health and it's because I'm healthy.' But Wanda does have regular medical check-ups: 'I go about once every two or three years. It costs a lot of money and I have an MOT check-up at a private hospital.'

National Health Service checks

Several interviewees mentioned the Well-Women and Well-Men clinics that their GP practices run that check such things as blood pressure, cholesterol levels and diabetes risk. Most of the interviewees were attending these. Although, as Maddy Lister pointed out, attendance is totally voluntary: 'It is not compulsory and you wonder whether perhaps it should be. It's just up to me to go along so if I didn't want to bother I wouldn't. I feel it's sensible though to actually be aware of your physical condition in terms of whether you need medication or not.'

Head in the sand approach

Not everyone is keen on having regular health checks and there were one or two interviewees who actively avoided them. Deirdre Goode was one: 'I don't go to the Well-Women check-ups. I think you'd only go if you thought that there was something the matter. And I'd rather not know! Probably a bit unwise.' Yes, I think that might be a bit unwise.

And while I think it's probably better to know, rather than not know, how do you cope with knowing, especially if it's serious? Barry and Anita Rudd talked about the modern trend of buying a full body scan. Anita: 'Barry's sister is buying her husband a full body scan for his 55th birthday. I said "Whatever for?" What's he going to do if he finds out he's got really early prostate cancer? Do you have it treated or do you wait a few years and see what happens?'

How old is too old for check-ups?

Amy Pillinger was on a drug trial which meant that she had very good check-ups for the duration of the trial: 'Unfortunately they've finished the trial now and going forward I won't get a lot of the tests any more because I'm older. You can go and request them from your GP but there's no guarantee that they'll do them. Things like mammograms usually stop at 67 whereas it is something that affects older women. I'd find a regular check-up very comforting.'

The combined wisdom on regular health checks

- If you had regular health checks when you were working, consider keeping them up.
- Attend your GP's 'Well-Women' or 'Well-Men' clinics, unless you want to take a 'head in the sand' approach.
- If your GP practice doesn't carry out some tests beyond a certain age, ask if you can have them anyway.

KEEPING MENTALLY ACTIVE

As an expert on the medical issues associated with ageing, Mary Edwards agrees that keeping physically active doesn't just help your body to remain healthy, it also helps your mind to stay healthy: 'There is some small evidence to suggest that physical activity delays the onset of dementia. But the trouble is that there are no longitudinal studies demonstrating that that's the case.' Over time, this is where the English Longitudinal Study of Ageing will help.

The study makes the point that the percentage of dementia in Western Europe before age 70 is low, around 1.5 per cent for ages 65 to 69. This rises gradually to 25 per cent for those aged 80+, so not everyone is going to develop dementia. However, the survey found that even those without dementia suffered a gradual decline in mental ability: memory, name-finding, complex decision making etc. We are led to believe that you can maintain and even improve your brain-power as you age. The Victorians believed that the brain, like the heart, was a muscle that required regular exercise to keep it fit and healthy. Recently, several books and television programmes have explored the theme of workouts for the brain and have extolled the benefits of using your mind in new and challenging ways as a means of warding off mental decline. So keeping mentally active may not stop you getting dementia but it might stop, or at least slow down, that gradual decline in mental ability.

Continuing to work

The pre-retirees who are working full time in stimulating jobs are deriving most of their current mental stimulation from the work they do. Consequently many of them see mental stimulation in retirement coming from continuing to be involved in business in some way. Gary Knight: 'I'd definitely like to stay in touch with business in some way. That's how I'd keep my brain sharp.'

Those transitional retirees who have kept a toe in the employment water are finding mental stimulation in continuing to work. While assignments are starting to tail off, Sean Jeffries enjoys the projects he still gets asked to work on and he wants to keep this going for a while: 'If I'm honest with myself I've said that I expect my work to run down but, every once in a while, I give it a little prod just to keep something going. I think I would be very happy if I could, over the next few years, periodically have an assignment and not cut it out completely.'

Sean is aware that once his assignments dry up he is going to need something to replace them: 'As the work drops away, keeping mentally active is going to become more important. I'll have to look for something inspiring to do with that aim in mind because otherwise I think if you let yourself slip mentally you are pretty well dead.'

One reason post-retiree Barry Rudd works with young companies is so that he remains mentally stimulated and challenged: 'On the business side some of the problems are quite tricky and that really makes you think. And you need to talk to people, talk about things to do with the business, and that also gets you thinking.'

And what have other post-retirees found that has inspired them, once their work has dried up? What do they do to keep mentally active? Colin Matthews deliberately tries to stretch himself with work-like activities: 'I get quite worried about my mental capacity waning and it's all the usual things like wanting something that's upstairs and I go upstairs and half-way up I think "Oh, while I'm up I'll just get so-and-so" and, of course, I get so-and-so and come down, having forgotten what I originally went up for. And my mother got Alzheimer's when she was 75 so I'm very much aware of it.' Colin's mixture of things to keep mentally active: 'I'm treasurer of the museum society, I'm an associate manager of a Mental Health NHS Trust, I'm in the local history society and I write books. It's doing things for groups and societies that keeps me mentally active. And all these activities give me a social outlet as well as a mental one.'

Several post-retirees agreed that being involved in groups, perhaps assisting with organizing things, helped to keep them alert and involved. William Kennett: 'Being involved in organizations is a huge help, mentally as well as socially.' And Ernest Dennis: 'Anything to do with the club, especially if you can help in some capacity.'

It seems to me that it's not just the actual work that post-retirees miss, it's also the stimulating and challenging social interaction with work colleagues. In spite of all his numerous post-retirement activities Sam Jarvis admits that, mentally, he misses his job: 'I feel myself that I'm not as bright as I used to be and I think that's because I miss work. You know, the round of meetings and all the things that came out of that.'

Being creative

But not everybody has the opportunity to continue to be involved in his or her pre-retirement career. Joan Jarvis's first career came to a sudden end and it wasn't until she was well into her 50s that she discovered her second career – creative embroidery and textiles. She is still passionate about what she does and claims that it is that that keeps her mind sharp: 'I have a project on all the time. I'm always working on exhibitions and trying to push myself that much further. And I'm always giving myself art challenges. So that's how I keep my mind active, it's active the entire time on what I'm going to be doing next, it never stops.' Having a passion certainly seems to work!

Continuing to be educated

After retirement, sharing the knowledge and wisdom we've acquired during our working lives by acting as mentors to young workers is of benefit to everyone involved. Carl Armstrong: 'Being the wise old head that's been round the block a few times, mentoring young professionals in the areas of my expertise, would be something that would be very rewarding, but it's finding the mechanism by which that could be done.'

Greg Eaton is mentoring for The Prince's Trust: 'At the moment it's just one youngster but if the opportunity arises I'd like to mentor another couple of guys. It's only an hour or two a month at the moment and it's very satisfying.' There are other mentoring opportunities available and a good scour of the internet should reveal several.

Continuing education

The idea of spending time in retirement learning new things appealed to several of the pre-retirees. The general feeling was that it would be good to learn something completely new and, even if it wasn't to degree standard, to learn in a structured way and environment. Nell Priest: 'I shall look into doing a new qualification. I'm not sure at this stage what it will be, or whether it will be to degree standard or not, but there's a part of me that thinks you do need to keep mentally active when you retire.'

Doing a degree, well, two in fact, is what helped Belinda Crompton make such a success of her post-retirement work on her land: 'Since then I have been trying to put it into practice so therefore everything I do physically also has a mental base for me to think about and it is part of a bigger picture.'

New pursuits

Not everyone wants to do a degree when they retire but the idea of learning something new inspired nearly all the pre-retirees. Maggie

Armstrong: 'I would like to take up something like bridge, something like that which I think would be good to learn and challenging. I'd rather do that than sign up to a university course.'

On the other hand, bridge is the last thing that Mary Edwards will be taking up: 'I detest card games, absolutely detest them.' What inspires Mary is the thought of doing history research: 'History research can be quite challenging if it's done properly.' She would like to research the history of her house in Norfolk.

When physical challenges provide mental stimulation

Belinda Crompton is convinced that the manual work she does challenges her mentally as well as physically. Brad Isles also talked about how physical activity encouraged mental activity: 'I think physical exercise, just walking for 10 miles, is a way of exercising your mind because you're observing things, you're taking things in and thinking about things all the time.'

An extreme-sports enthusiast, post-retiree Sam Jarvis knows all about the importance of getting it right, both mentally and physically: 'I fly a micro-light. It doesn't flavour one's pleasure of it but you are aware of the fact that, if you get it wrong, you're in deep trouble. You're responsible for everything, from preparing the thing to flying it around, talking on the radio and so on. That gives you lots to do and you make sure that you get it right, most of the time anyway!'

Reading

Reading was the most popular activity, for both pre- and post-retirees, for helping them to keep mentally challenged. In spite of the time spent working and commuting Brad Isles is an avid reader; this is what his wife, Julie, says: 'Brad reads all the time. He reads much more learned books than me, he's almost constantly reading.' Sean Jeffries on reading: 'I find I get a lot of mental stimulus from reading. And I do try, I'm trying now, to widen my repertoire of what I read.'

James and Denise Dent have some good friends, Bob and Ann, who are their retiree role models, and who read a lot. James: 'Reading is important. I'm still very interested in lots of things, history and that kind of thing. Looking to people like Bob and Ann, they're full of books and we're always exchanging books with them or picking up ideas for books.'

And Mary Edwards, our expert on ageing-related issues: 'I do always read novels. I've always got a novel on the go. I enjoy reading most of all, whether it keeps your brain good I don't know. There's no evidence that keeping mentally active will have any impact on keeping you free of dementia.' But while keeping mentally active might not keep you free of dementia it might help to stop, or at least delay, that mental decline which the English Longitudinal Study of Ageing discovered happens with older people.

Belonging to a book group and being encouraged to read books you might not normally read, and then discuss them, is very popular. Belinda Crompton has belonged to a book group for the past 35 years: 'You get to know people in a completely different way within the book group, how they think and why they think and so it's very useful, both socially and mentally.'

For Maddy Lister reading is a part of her recipe for keeping mentally active, although, rather amusingly: 'I now make lists of the books I've read because I keep forgetting the titles, the authors and when I read them!'

Keeping up with current affairs

Most pre-retirees said that they regarded keeping up with current affairs mentally stimulating and is something that they would want to keep on doing. Carl Armstrong: 'Things of general ongoing background interest, things like current affairs, that's something that I have an interest in, and I would want that to keep rolling on.' The post-retirees agreed but several said that as they got older they found the situation in the world, and the constant media reporting of it, depressing. Maddy Lister: 'I like to keep abreast of current affairs. I think that came from my father who even on his death-bed was interested in what was happening in the world. It was absolutely amazing, when he was in hospital with his terminal illness he wanted to know what the stock market was doing! I do watch the news albeit I don't watch it quite as much as I used to because I find it incredibly disheartening.'

Young company

Keeping company with young people is one of the ways in which Deirdre Goode keeps mentally stimulated: 'I like talking to young people. I do like young ideas and things, it's great when they're around. A lot of my friends are younger than me because I'm an older mother and they're friends that I've made through my children's schools. In fact two of my friends have got quite young children. I think it does help to keep me bright and alert.'

William Kennett agrees with Deirdre and believes that having a younger wife helps: 'I think I'm lucky. If there are two of you who are my age it's much more difficult. I think having someone 23 years younger than yourself keeps you mentally active.'

The performing arts

Those interviewees who play a musical instrument find learning a new piece a great way to keep mentally alert. Pre-retiree Nell Priest is a very accomplished pianist but raised an interesting point:

> I'm sort of dithering about whether I will continue to play the piano after I retire, that will be a test of my resolve. At the moment I have so much on as well as finding time to do my piano practice. When I retire and I don't have quite so much stuff going on, para-doxically I think I will have to be doubly motivated to keep my practice up. But I do enjoy playing and I'm sure it will help to keep me mentally alert.

Sam Jarvis is in no doubt that playing the organ keeps him up to scratch: 'One of the things that I do is to try and learn a new and diffi-cult organ piece, that really keeps me stretched!'

The other thing that Sam believes keeps him stretched mentally is preparing for and presenting the talks that he gives on cruise ships: 'Depending on the trip I prepare a new lecture. That involves putting a PowerPoint presentation together and things like that and it's pretty interesting and demanding.'

Ernest Dennis agrees with Sam that giving talks has helped him to keep his mind active and exploring: 'Writing a speech about some-thing or giving a talk, that's an excellent way to keep alert.'

Crosswords and Sudoku

Wow! I wasn't ready for the passions that such innocent pursuits could arouse in my interviewees. Very few of the interviewees were doing Sudoku, most just don't see the point, and Sarah Joyce is one of them: 'I don't like Sudoku in the sense that I think it's a time-waster. I don't think you learn anything. I wouldn't want a pointless activity.' Mary Edwards: 'I'm definitely not going to do Sudoku!'

On the other hand, crosswords had more of a following from both pre- and post-retirees. Anita Rudd: 'I often fight Barry for the crossword, they do say that doing crosswords is a good thing.'

And James Dent: 'At the end of each day Denise and I sit down with the *Telegraph* crossword and have a go at that. The days we finish it are very cheerful and those we can't do it we are very miserable but it's that sort of hour in the evening when we just get the white wine out and have a go.'

Helen Kennett: 'We do the crosswords.' William added: 'With the aid of the atlas, the thesaurus, the dictionary and any other book that we can call to our attention!'

Interaction

Time and again, whatever people were doing to keep themselves mentally active, we came back to the importance of interaction between people. Interaction seemed to be a common element in virtually all of the mental activities, whether it was Belinda Crompton's book club, Craig Armstrong's mentoring, Sean Jeffries and others' continuation of work, even doing the crossword seems to provide more stimulation if you are doing it with someone else. As Sean Jeffries says: 'I like something that involves interaction, that's the thing that I have really, really enjoyed about the work I used to do.' So, it would appear that keeping mentally active is also about keeping socially active.

Or do none of the above!

As controversial as ever, Wanda Purcell had a different take on keeping mentally active:

I do *The Times* crossword every day. I don't finish it every day, maybe once a week. I don't read books for improvement, I read them for escape. I read a lot but it's novels. I've never attended an adult education class in my life. All my friends, oh my goodness, they learn Italian, they go to pottery classes, I can't tell you what they do. I do none of that. I can't be bothered with any of it. I don't feel any need to learn anything, it's very self-satisfying isn't it? So all these people who set themselves up for mental challenges, either creative or intellectual, just not my cup of tea.

Wanda really is the exception that proves the rule but as she says growing older is about being content in your own skin: 'And part of being old is not having to feel guilty about not doing it, even if every-body else is doing it at 80. I don't need to compare myself with other people and feel a failure because I'm not learning Italian. It's perfectly all right to be as I am.' And I have to agree, she is perfectly all right as she is!

The combined wisdom of keeping mentally active

- Keeping mentally active might not stop you getting dementia but it might help to delay the onset of the decline in mental ability that comes as you age.
- If you derive mental stimulation from work-like activities, find a retirement occupation that will re-create that.
- Post-retirees don't just miss work, they miss the stimulation that the social interaction with their work colleagues provided. Many found an adequate replacement in joining groups and organizations and becoming involved in these by helping or contributing in some way.
- Find a passion and follow it.
- Become a mentor of young people.
- Learn something new.
- If learning for learning's sake doesn't appeal, think about what you might learn that would help you do other things that you want to do better.
- Challenging yourself physically can also stimulate mental activity.
- Read more.
- Keep up to speed with current affairs.
- Keep the company of younger people.
- Stretch and challenge yourself in an existing activity.
- Do crosswords (or Sudoku!).
- Keep socially active.
- Don't be bullied into doing any of the above!

YOU ARE WHAT YOU EAT

We keep being told that it is one of the paradoxes of modern life: more cookery books are sold and less home cooking is done than ever before. But I was impressed by the amount of vegetable growing, cooking from scratch and general attention to diet that is going on among the interviewees. Here's just a small sample:

I certainly tailor the diet for healthier living. I've grown vegetables in our plot always and we have been here for 25 years now. I do try and eat properly.

Joan Jarvis

We grow a lot of our own vegetables and much of what we eat is made at home anyway, from all the bread that's baked and everything else, so we do eat healthily.

James Dent

I do try and cook healthy food and lots of fruit and veg and not too much fat and not too much red meat.

Samantha Jeffries

Now don't think that we eat chips and all that, I mean dieting has played a big part. Not strict diets but we try to be sensible. We eat a lot of fruit. We don't have puddings as much as we used to.

Ernest Dennis

But don't get too hung up about it!

In spite of the many dietary virtues I noted very few people were beating themselves up if they gave in to the occasional temptation:

I don't worry too much about it. I mean I try. I eat possibly too much. I enjoy food but as long as I get enough nourishment I am not fussy about it. I grow things as far as I can myself but part of that's the pleasure of doing it as much as thinking "Oh, I can't put that in my body" or whatever.

Belinda Crompton

Around the edges I'm good when it comes to what I eat but I have to say I am partial to the odd cream cake.

Michelle Stansfield

I do try and eat fish mainly but sometimes, just sometimes I succumb to a steak.

Brad Isles

Is wanting to look good the preserve of the young?

Not according to some of the people I interviewed. Nell Priest admitted that her chief motivation for paying attention to her diet isn't to preserve her health but to preserve her figure:

I'm not neurotic about my diet in the sense that I think I should avoid certain foods because they are going to give me a heart attack. It's more to do with physical appearance. I am neurotic about my weight and that's something that I think most women share. And I resent it but at the same time it has to be said that if you spend your entire life finding that some clothes look better on you thinner then you worry about your diet.

Wanda Purcell's concerns over her appearance made her go to Weightwatchers: 'Three years ago I knew that I was overweight, and that was because I didn't like the look of myself. It wasn't because I was huffing and puffing. I just didn't like the look of myself. And so I went to Weightwatchers and did everything I was told and lost two stones.'

Drinking

Alcohol consumption centred around wine, with most of the interviewees admitting that they enjoyed more than the occasional glass. But the belief that drinking on your own is the thin end of the wedge has certainly hit home with some of the interviewees who live alone.

'I probably drink a bottle of wine a week and maybe another couple of glasses, but I wouldn't drink more than that. I think when you are on your own you have to be quite careful about that.' – Deirdre Goode

And those who live alone don't usually have a partner who can take turns to drink/drive. Michelle Stansfield: 'I don't drink much because everywhere I go I drive. I've practically become teetotal. Occasionally when I go out I will have one, but I never, ever drink at home. I decided after Graham died that I wouldn't drink at home because I was frightened that if I did it might be the start of the slippery slope.'

Some of the pre- and transitional retirees say they drink more because of the pressure of their jobs and consequently alcohol consumption will drop when they retire. Brad Isles: 'I come home from work and drinking wine is a release. I circle round the kitchen and Julie is doing the cooking and we're talking and I'm drinking and unwinding. But when I'm not working and I'm doing all those other things that I plan to do, then this won't be a release, it will just be a bit of a bonus at the end of the day, and I think I will drink less.'

Who's buying organic?

Some interviewees are buying organic but mostly only where they think it makes a difference. And there were several cynics. Sean Jeffries was typical: 'I think a lot of food producers can make a lot of money out of the organic label and continue to grow things in much the same way as they always did. So I pick and choose. I wouldn't buy organic asparagus but I might buy organic chicken.'

But being cynical doesn't always stop us buying! Wanda Purcell: 'If I have a choice in a supermarket between organic and non-organic I'm the sucker that pays more for the stuff that they label organic, although it probably isn't.'

How important are food miles?

Several interviewees were concerned about how far food had come at the cost of lost food value and expense to the environment, and tried to buy locally rather than organically. Julie Isles: 'I tend to buy local farm stuff and I try and avoid anything that comes from a long way away. I would sooner buy farm carrots from Evesham than organic carrots from Egypt.'

Vicky Alder agrees: 'I do like to shop locally but it doesn't have to be organic, as long as it's not flown miles. It's the first thing I look at, it's not whether it's organic but from whence it came.'

But as Richard Jeffries says: 'The most important thing is what it tastes like.'

Who's taking supplements?

Some of the interviewees are taking supplements: cod liver oil, vitamins C and D and glucosamine are the favourites. But cynicism as to how effective they are is rife and some of it is informed cynicism. As an eminent doctor and researcher, part of Richard Jeffries' job is to be aware of the results of various health studies. The Jeffries don't believe in taking supplements; Samantha's view is you don't need to if you have a healthy diet. Richard takes it a step further: 'Vitamin supplements are seriously detrimental. For a million people who take vitamin supplements one thousand of them will suffer premature death, did you know that? No seriously. There was a very large random survey on vitamin supplementation so, providing they're not beneficial for anything, then one in a thousand will die early.'

Mary Edwards, another medical expert whose job it is to keep abreast of the results of medical surveys, took supplements for a while: 'I used to take vitamins A, C and E, because I thought there was some vague benefit and then a whole bunch of new research came out that says it's a load of rubbish so I gave that up.'

However, Mary does take one pill regularly: 'I take an aspirin every day. I think there is enough evidence to show the benefit of doing that.' Although, as she points out, taking an aspirin every day could have potentially damaging side effects and it isn't a replacement for doing all the other good things one should be doing: 'The most important thing for strokes is to keep your blood pressure down and your cholesterol down and that, or course, is helped by diet and exercise.' So, there's no getting away from the diet and exercise!

Most of those who are taking supplements admitted that they didn't know how effective they were. As Wanda Purcell says: 'For years and years I've taken cod liver oil because it's supposed to ease the joints. As I don't have any pain in my joints it presumably is effective but of course you don't know, do you? If you have a headache and take an aspirin you don't know if the headache would have gone away anyway, without the aspirin.'

What does Mr Misery have to say?

Well, he takes a pretty analytical approach. Carl Armstrong: 'I shall maintain current dietary habits, linked with gradually reducing food intake, because you are losing 2.3 per cent of your muscle mass every year and therefore even if you stay fit you just need less energy to maintain the body mass that you have.' Golly, that sounds like a tall order and his wife, Maggie, agrees: 'To actually get round to reducing it though does seem a bit ambitious.'

The combined wisdom of you are what you eat

- Eat wisely but don't get hung up about it, the occasional dietary sin is good.
- Grow your own vegetables, for the fun as much as for the dietary benefits.
- Cook from scratch.
- Women worry about their body shape all through their lives.
- Alcohol consumption depends on where you are in your life.
- Most people are cynical about organic food but it doesn't stop them buying it, although several are selective about it.
- Food miles are important, buy local if possible.
- Supplements may not be all they're cracked up to be.
- Mr Misery says that we should all be reducing our food intake as we grow older.

WHO HAS PRIVATE MEDICAL INSURANCE?
Private medicine v NHS when something goes wrong

Having been a doctor all his life, if Richard Jeffries needed medical attention he simply picked up the phone to one of his mates: 'But now, of course, I can't do that. At least I can do it less and less because many of my friends are retired so you become more and more a non-person and that is something I'm not used to. I am used to the fact that if I wanted something medically someone would say "Yes of course I'll see you tomorrow." '

Richard and Samantha Jeffries have never had private medical insurance and like many people in their situation are happy to self-insure on the basis that the NHS is at its best when it comes to treating serious conditions; where it tends to fall down is dealing with the more minor complaints that aren't life threatening. Samantha explained: 'I feel that if I needed a new knee suddenly I'd rather pay for it than pay insurance for it and financially we can afford to do that.'

When William Kennett said to his specialist: 'I think you'll agree with me that if you're really ill the best thing to do is have National Health the specialist did agree but went on to say: 'If you've got a hernia and you have private medical insurance I can get you in within three days rather than the three months it would take with the NHS.' Or, presumably, if you don't have insurance but can afford to pay.

On the other hand, Belinda Crompton has private medical insurance and was grateful for the cover it gave her when she was ill a few years ago, but says: 'I would have been fine, I am sure, under the National Health Service as well and I'm now back in that system for my check-ups. But it's reassuring to know that I have private medical insurance for things like hips or knees or whatever, private medical treatment is good for speed of getting things done.'

Self-insurance

Rather than taking out private medical insurance the Armstrongs have decided to self-insure. Maggie explains: 'We've set aside a pot of money to cover potential future cost of medical treatment. If we don't need it then it's available to spend on other things. There should be enough money around, we would hope, for most things.'

Several interviewees have self-insured, especially when they've found out how much private medical insurance costs. Sean Jeffries thinks that the NHS works well and he's happy to self-insure for the things that might take longer for the NHS to deal with:

We have an extremely good NHS hospital down the road. I had an occasion to use it recently, just for minor things, and it was fantastic. Where private medical insurance is helpful is if you've got some persistent condition where you would have to wait a long time for the NHS to deal with it. I used to have private medical insurance but it was going to cost quite a lot to keep it going so I decided to self-insure.

If you feel comfortable self-insuring you might want to consider ring-fencing a pot of money, maybe just notionally, that you regard as your own personal medical emergencies' pot. But do bear in mind that even quite simple procedures can be expensive, so you might want to talk to a financial planner about the types and cost of private medical insurance available.

Increasing cost of private medical insurance

Several interviewees who have private medical insurance have done the sums and know that they haven't, as yet, had their money's worth. Wanda Purcell: 'I've got it but I've never had to use it. And the cost keeps going up. Golly they've made money out of me! Have they made money!'

The cost of private medical insurance does keep going up as you get older but the chances of making a claim increase too. If you have private medical insurance you need to weigh up the potential future cost/benefit. Deirdre Goode is in this situation: 'I do have private medical insurance and it's quite expensive and the older you get the worse it becomes. I think I'll keep it going because I've gone down that route. I think you either buy medical insurance or you save for it and I haven't done that. I wouldn't like to rely solely on my own funds and the NHS.'

Company cover and 'continuation of cover'

Some of the pre-retirees have private medical insurance as part of their employment package, often covering spouse and children. Several of the transitional and post-retirees have kept the cover going after leaving work. Sometimes, under a 'continuation of cover' option, it is possible to do this on favourable terms. Nell Priest intends to keep her private medical cover she has with her firm when she retires: 'I think it's negotiable to keep it. I believe that you can be in a sort of sub-set of retired members of the firm which I intend to do because it's still a good deal.'

William Kennett has a good deal with his previous employer; even though he has been retired for 17 years they still pay half of the premium for his private medical insurance policy.

Certainly deals like this make the cost of private medical insurance more affordable.

What is and isn't covered

Some of the conditions associated with old age are not covered by private medical insurance. Whether the insurance companies will review their stance on this as more of the population live to greater ages remains to be seen, and if they do, no doubt the cost will rise. Maddy Lister was frustrated that her private medical policy couldn't help with the treatment for her hearing loss: 'I have private medical insurance but I haven't actually used it. Well, I did try and use it for the recent implant that I had into my skull for a fitting of a particular kind of hearing aid but they weren't interested. I couldn't claim. They don't do anything to do with hearing aids so I haven't claimed anything.'

Chronic conditions aren't usually covered either. Chronic conditions are ailments that you had before taking out private medical insurance and are unlikely to get better; one example is diabetes. Gary Knight has two chronic conditions. He has private medical insurance through his employment and it covers all the family: 'The two complaints I've got aren't covered because our health insurance won't cover anything that's chronic so in my case it's of limited value. But Gloria and the children have made great use of it over the last few years.'

A word of warning

This is by no means an objective review of the benefits or otherwise of private medical insurance, it is simply reporting the views and experiences of the interviewees. And it certainly isn't a comprehensive review of private medical policies, of which there are many and varied ones. If you are considering taking out private medical insurance, ask a professional adviser who is qualified to advise on all policies.

If you have a private medical insurance policy and are considering cancelling it, think long and hard. Cancelling an existing policy is fraught with potential difficulties; there's the worry that you might tempt providence and the moment you lose the cover a medical disaster strikes. And if you decide it was the wrong move to cancel the policy, there is the problem of reapplying for cover with potentially increased premiums, and conditions that were previously covered now excluded.

The combined wisdom on private medical insurance

■   The general feeling amongst the interviewees is that the NHS is fine if you've got a serious problem but not so good if your problem isn't life threatening because of the waiting times for treatment.

■   If you can afford to ring-fence a sum of money for your private medical costs then consider self-insuring.

■   But medical costs can be large so make sure you can ring-fence enough.

■   If self-insurance doesn't appeal, or won't work for you, talk to a financial planner about the different types of private medical insurance available and the potential cost and see if there is one to suit you.

■   If you're in a company private medical insurance scheme, check if you can keep the cover on after you've retired.

■   If you already have private medical insurance, or are considering taking it out, check exactly what is and isn't covered. And check out the monetary maximums for any treatment.

■   If you are considering taking out private medical insurance and have a pre-existing condition, check how the insurance company will deal with this.

FINALLY...

The cards might just be stacked against you

Of course you can do everything right – eat healthily, exercise and have regular medical checks and still get sick. As Gary Knight points out: 'I'm a firm believer that you can be physically fit, mentally fit and you can eat all the right things, but all of a sudden something comes out of the blue, some illness.' Agreed, but surely it's sensible to hedge your bets and look after your health, then even if life does bowl you a googly and you get sick at least you're in better condition to deal with it.

And you might just be lucky

Several of the interviewees admitted that they were so lucky with their health that they took it for granted. Complacency can be as dangerous as obsession: 'I think we're alarmingly casual about maintaining our health because we've been very lucky and just take it all for granted.' – James Dent

Gloria Knight summed it up by pointing out that one shouldn't get too hung up on anything – just have a good time: 'I think if you're enjoying what you're doing that's more important than anything. I think if you've get some pleasure out of life, if you get up in the morning and think: "Thank you God, it's another day," you can't ask for more than that.'

4

Care in later old age

'Ultimately we will need to think about making some arrangements for our long-term care and need to have a mechanism in place to know exactly what we're going to do before the time comes.'

Sean Jeffries

No one wants to think about being in advanced old age and needing help with basic daily functions. Nearly every person I interviewed, young and old, was taking the ostrich approach to the issue and burying their heads in the sand. Immediate reactions to my questions about plans for care in old age ran along these lines:

'Well, I think about it occasionally then I rapidly think about something else!'
'Head in the sand about it really. I've given it no thought whatsoever.'
'If I'm being really honest I avoid even thinking about it.'
'We put that off – we push it behind us.'

Are they taking such a cavalier attitude because they're the younger interviewees? Far from it, the last quote is from Diane Dennis who is 76.

The people I interviewed are not alone in their approach. Help the Aged recently carried out a survey of 942 adults between the ages of 45 and 65 and found that two-thirds had made no provision whatsoever for future care.

Why don't people want to think about that later period of their lives, let alone plan for it? Well, there's the attitude of: life's too short and it won't happen to me. And yet statistical evidence seems to indicate that there is a strong chance that it will. The Joseph Rowntree Foundation has produced a report entitled 'Future Demand for Long Term Care in the UK'. According to the report the number of people aged 85 and over is set to grow from 1.1m in 2000 to 4m in 2051. Currently around 40 per cent of people aged 85 and over receive residential care before they die and this percentage is set to rise as people's life expectancy increases.

Another barrier to planning is that most people have a negative view of care homes. Mary Edwards, who has worked in the health service at a high level, specializing in ageing-related conditions, has indicated in every formal document she can lay her hands on that she never wants to be admitted to a care home. When I asked her why, her response was: 'Generally my experience of residential or nursing homes, when I've been visiting them in the course of my work, has been very negative – very.'

Wanda Purcell's rather bleak view of care homes: 'My mental picture of an old people's home is of Rexene chairs round the edge of the room, the backs are to the wall and there's a television permanently on soaps or horror things. I don't look forward to it. I'm rather hoping money may again come to the rescue and it won't actually be Rexene chairs around the room, they'll be in some sort of rose-tinted brocade.' In Wanda's case money may indeed come to the rescue because she is well off, but not everyone is.

How likely are you to need care?

Perhaps the primary reason people put off thinking about, and planning for, the care stage of their lives is because they have no idea when, or even if, the event will happen and how it will happen. As Ernest Dennis says: 'You're either going to go gaga or incontinent.' – pleasant choices, no wonder no one wants to think about it!

Well, you may be lucky and never need care – you might die with your boots on so to speak. On the other hand, the medical profession's ability to prolong life at a greater rate than it is prolonging the capacity to operate as an independent individual may just catch you out – euthanasia is still not a legal option! With his usual happy outlook, Carl Armstrong, aka Mr Misery, did have a take on this: 'You can only go on for so long and we may get to a stage where you can just be left out on a cold winter's night; you'd just go to sleep and you'd never wake up. Now, is that really so terrible, because that's what the Inuit do.' Mmmm, not sure I fancy it; though, faced with that and the Rexene chairs, it's a close call, but I think the chairs win out.

The findings of the Joseph Rowntree Foundation report indicate that the chances are pretty high that you will need care. Chances are also pretty high you'll have to pay for it because, faced with growing demand, the government is unlikely to be able to pay very much towards the cost of providing care; the size and needs of an ageing population will simply overwhelm the Exchequer.

If you need care, what's available?

I am totally discounting possible help from friends and relatives. The care system currently available in this country would collapse overnight without the help and support of 'carers', close relatives and friends who give their time to care for others. But everyone I have ever spoken to on the issue has said that if they need care in old age, the last thing they want to do is to rely on family help; it just puts too much strain on relationships and can mar several lives.

Richard Jeffries spoke for most parents when he said: 'I think that the most important thing is not to be a financial and organizational burden on our daughters. I don't mean to say that they shouldn't pay any attention to us at all but simply that they haven't got to dig into their own savings and too much of their own time in order to help us.'

I am also discounting sheltered accommodation because generally people who enter such accommodation are reasonably mobile and independent. It is worth mentioning, though, that some sheltered accommodation, sometimes referred to as 'extra care sheltered housing', does have more comprehensive care facilities within the same compound so that a resident can progress through the system if their condition deteriorates. Amy Pillinger knows of one such facility: 'There's a complex near me which is very good. It has bungalows where you can live totally independently then you can buy in help as you need it. There are restaurant and catering facilities available and a nursing home so you can progress through the system, which is quite far seeing, I think.'

Being cared for in their own homes is an option that almost everyone I spoke to would prefer, accepting that if their medical needs were severe this might not be possible. Richard Jeffries again: 'Ideally to be cared for in our own home for as long as possible. But it depends on your mental faculties and your physical faculties. Certain conditions are so varied that it's very difficult to predict how we would be. But both of us would say that what we'd rather do is keep our independence for as long as possible.' However, home care is not a cheap option. The cost of care in your own home, or domiciliary care as it is sometimes called, can be more expensive than care in a residential or nursing home.

If being cared for in your own home isn't an option, there are two types of care home available: residential and nursing. Residential homes are for people who are relatively well but need help with some daily activities, and nursing homes are for people who need a greater degree of nursing care.

Several people I talked to, particularly transitional retirees, had a theory about communal living; the basic idea being that as they got older they would club together with a group of friends, buy a big house, employ a qualified staff to look after them and live and be cared for in that community until they died. This is one up from the 'retirement village' concept.

Sean Jeffries on this issue: 'What's to stop you buying a place, getting some friends in and saying this is where we are going to be. Stick a stair lift up the stairs, you know, job done!'

Others weren't too sure about this approach. Nell Priest: 'We'll all end up pureeing each other's cabbage – ghastly thought!' The commune approach obviously isn't everyone's cup of tea – or pureed cabbage.

I am a great believer in the power of the baby boomers to change things. As Sean Jeffries says: 'The baby boomers are coming up against the issue of care and just as we've been noisy and disruptive in everything else, we're bound to be noisy and disruptive in that.' I do believe that the baby boomers will change, for the better, the way that older people are cared for in the UK, but whatever changes are brought about it will take time and, if you want choice, there is still likely to be a financial cost.

What is the potential cost of care?

Well, that depends on the quality of the care home you are in and the length of time you spend there between entering and dying – sounds harsh, but that's the reality.

There are also regional differences in the cost of care homes. For example, the average cost of a single room in a residential home in Greater London is £26,000 per annum. The same accommodation in the north of England would cost, on average, £19,000 per annum.

Nursing homes are more expensive. The average cost of a single room in a nursing home in Greater London is £38,000 per annum compared with £25,000 in the north of England.

And remember that these are average costs – if you want something above average it will cost you more. Colin Matthews is not sure that he will be able to afford a home with rose-tinted brocade and that he'll end up at the mercy of the local authority: 'Whether I was happy with that would depend on which retirement home they put me into. I don't want a smelly one.' He would like to think that by the time he needs care there will be more resources available from the local authority but this is unlikely.

And the cost of care homes is increasing at a greater rate than inflation. Average care home fees have been increasing by 7 to 8 per cent per annum. In fact, according to Laing and Buisson, an independent company providing authoritative data, there has been a 50 per cent increase in yearly fees for nursing homes between 2000 and 2006.

How do I know which are good and which are not so good care homes?

The Commission for Social Care Inspection (CSCI) has introduced a new way of grading care homes with a star grading system, a bit like hotels, 1 star for poor, up to 3 for excellent. However, like hotel gradings, you might disagree with the Commission's findings. Its website at www.csci.org.uk is worth looking at. You will find a link to the report on the home page under 'Find a Care Service or Care Home'.

By far and away the best way to assess a care home is to visit it. Initially most of us will experience care homes second hand, perhaps when we are helping parents select a home or visiting a relative or friend. Sean Jeffries was pleased that he had had an opportunity to visit several nursing homes when he was helping his mother choose a home:

My mother is certainly in a good care home and there are others. We saw networks of homes when we were looking for a place for my mother, and thought they were extremely good because they allowed you to continue to have a certain amount of independence and associate with like-minded people. And they had nice facilities, whilst at the same time providing you with the nursing care, and other such care you might need, at the rate and pace at which you need it.

So it might be worth paying a visit to some local care homes – or at least sounding friends and family out about their experience of what's available locally.

What's the average length of stay in a care home?

The average length of stay in a care home between entry and death is commonly thought to be in the region of two to three years. However, Partnership Assurance believes that this is an underestimate; according to it, in 2002 an 87-year-old woman going into a care home would be expected to have survived for four years and eight months. In 2006 this increased to five years and four months, an annual increase of 4 per cent.

Will lengths of stay in care homes continue to increase at the same rate? Hard to predict as it will depend on many factors, including continued affluence, advances in medical treatments, government ability to help with funding, etc.

The point to note here is that when you are working out the likely cost of care in old age it would be dangerous to underestimate how long your period of residence in a care home will be – again, you may not be average. It is unthinkable that an elderly and frail person could be evicted from a care home because they couldn't pay the fees, but in reality that is what might happen if they run out of money.

What financial help is available?

State funding for long-term care falls into two categories – nursing and social. Nursing care is provided by the NHS and social care is provided by the local authority. And it all ought to run smoothly but it doesn't, in fact it's a bit of a mess.

There is no countrywide method of determining whether someone qualifies for full nursing care. The Department of Health admits that from 1996 to 2003 there were over 90 different sets of local criteria used to decide whether people were eligible for NHS support. Since 2003 local criteria have been set by the Strategic Health Authorities – of which there are only 28!

What help is available for social care is also a bit of a lottery and even when basic State care is available, it is just that – basic. It is also means tested. If you have assets (2008 figures) in excess of a certain sum (£22,250 in England and Northern Ireland, £22,000 in Wales and £21,500 in Scotland), you will receive no help with care costs at all. If your assets are below a certain sum (£13,500 in England and Northern

Ireland, £19,000 in Wales and £13,000 in Scotland), the local authority is obliged to provide you with accommodation but this could be the cheapest available in the country, possibly in a shared room too.

There are moves afoot by the government to standardize its approach to care provision but this will take time. To find out more about NHS-funded nursing care and local authority social care, visit www.dh.gov.uk. Age Concern also has an excellent website at www.ace.org.uk that provides good information about available benefits.

I wouldn't bank on the NHS, or the local authorities, being able to dig deeper into their coffers as time goes by and provide more to help with the cost of care. According to the Joseph Rowntree Foundation report, long-term care expenditure needs to rise by around 315 per cent in real terms between 2000 and 2015, the equivalent of 1.8 per cent of GDP. For most people that will mean self-funding, as the government, facing ever-larger care bills, is unlikely to pick up the tab.

My advice to those wishing to make some prior provision for care fees is to assume that there will be no State help available whatsoever – you are on your own. If some financial help is available when you need care, then it will be a bonus.

What's the best way to make provision for the potential cost of long-term care?

Part of the problem of making provision for something that isn't going to happen until some unknown date in the future, and may not happen at all, is that you do not know how much provision to make.

It is well worth working with a financial planner who can help you prepare some long-term projections, based on sensible assumptions, to try to quantify the potential cost of long-term care. Having quantified the sum, the simplest and most flexible approach to making provision is to discount the sum back to today's terms. Then, using an assumed growth rate, between now and the assumed date of going into a care home, estimate how much you would have to ring-fence or invest now to provide you with your future care costs.

Often the ring-fencing is just notional; in other words, you mentally earmark a particular asset or investment as your long-term care fund and, as such, it is not to be used for other purposes. The asset must, of course, have the potential for growing in value at the rate assumed in your calculation. For example, you might have a holiday home that you regard as your long-term care fund. If you have to sell it before you need to go into care, you invest in another asset earmarked in the same way. Alternatively, you might notionally earmark a portion of your investments as your long-term care fund.

Another approach would be to set up a regular savings plan that you regard as your long-term care savings plan. Or determine that when you retire and receive the tax-free cash lump sum from your pension you will invest and earmark part of this for future care fees.

The advantage of these approaches is that if you never need to pay for care you still have the money. A further advantage of making prior provision in this way is that it gives peace of mind. You know that, bar accidents, you have the wherewithal to pay for care. It means that you can relax about spending the rest of your money, or giving it away to reduce your inheritance tax bill! It means that you are able to feel confident that you can leave money to your children. And it means that you don't become one of those people who deprive themselves of treats because they are frightened that they may need the money later on to pay for long-term care – you've already put the money on one side.

What about using the value tied up in your home to pay for care fees?

A growing number of people are considering using the value in their homes to pay for their care fees; Sean Jeffries is one: 'Paying for care is going to be a challenge and this is where this house comes in, it pays for that or its heirs and successors do.'

Chapter 8, on equity release, explains how it is possible to unlock the value tied up in your home. Using equity release to fund long-term care fees can be cost effective. This is because when you go into care you are likely to have a reduced life expectancy and, as such, could be given preferential rates by the equity release company. However, this is only likely to be effective if you are a couple, with one of you remaining in the home.

Can insurance help?

It can, but only in a limited way. The long-term care insurance market is in disarray and most of the policies that were used for prior funding for care fees have been removed from the shelves. Over time, I think that this part of the insurance market will get its act together and we might have some worthwhile offerings, but it will take time.

The policies that are available at point of need, called immediate-needs annuities, have more to recommend them and, when you get to that stage, you might want to consider using some of your long-term care fund to buy one. They work as follows: when someone enters a care home a lump sum is used to buy an annuity. The annuity payments are made, tax-free, direct to the care provider. The annuity is medically underwritten so someone in poor health will have to pay less than someone in good health. As most people going into care are not in good health, immediate-needs annuities can be good value, especially if you outlive the medical underwriters' expectations! There are various options available with these annuities, so research and understanding are crucial. As always, the overriding priority is to make sure that the annuity chosen will continue to pay the chosen care home's fees until the annuitant dies.

It is also possible to take out an immediate-needs annuity that ensures that payments are made to agencies that provide care in the home. They are usually fully portable, so if you fall out with the care provider you can switch to another one.

Protecting the family home

I am often asked about the use of the family home in long-term care planning.

I have seen varying statistics on how many homes have to be sold each year to pay for long-term care, figures varying from 40,000 to 70,000, but, whatever the number, it's a large one.

I do appreciate that people get hot under the collar when they have worked hard and saved and are denied means-tested State benefits because they have too many assets. But that's the way the system works, and would you want to deprive yourself of assets just to qualify for means-tested benefits? Would you want to receive the basic level of social care in old age?

There are lots of clever schemes around, using the family home in an attempt to put this asset out of the reach of the assessment for benefits system. The government doesn't like it and is doing everything in its power to stop it, so beware if you are planning to use such a scheme. The local authorities have powers under the 'deliberate deprivation rule' to examine whether an asset was given away in the full knowledge that it might be needed sometime in the future to pay for care fees and, if it was, to treat it as if it had never been given away and use it in their assessment process.

Houses are used when assessing someone's assets for means-tested benefits. But there are some occasions when the house is excluded. The house is excluded if the following person or persons lives there:

■ a partner, married or unmarried;
■ a relative over 60;
■ a disabled relative;
■ a dependent child under 16;
■ a former partner who is divorced or estranged from you but who is a lone parent.

There is also discretion to ignore if:

■ the house is occupied by a carer who gave up their own home to care; or
■ the care is being provided on a temporary basis.

There is a 12-week property disregard, which means that the property will be disregarded for the first 12 weeks of needing permanent care provided that the other capital is below the upper means-test limit; see earlier in this chapter under 'What financial help is available?' for details of the means-tested limits.

If the home is assessable because none of the above exemptions apply, the government operates a deferred payment agreement for homes. If the property remains unsold, the local authority will continue to pay towards the care fees but this money is repayable once the home is sold. It does not charge interest on the money.

The next big thing – when's the right time to go into care?

As everyone I spoke to couldn't bear to think about the prospect of needing care, no one is considering taking the plunge too soon. But there is sense in not leaving it too late. Wanda Purcell has always admired her mother's approach to going into care:

My mother was totally sensible. When she saw the time coming and could no longer look after herself, she said: 'Wanda, it's time we looked for an old people's home,' and she did it whilst she could still cope with it. I just hope I will be like her and say: 'Nice time to go and look at old people's homes.' In other words, while one can still make choices. I think I'll be quite good at not clinging on, to the detriment of my family and friends, but will say: 'All right, now we've got to do the next thing.'

Also, delaying thinking about and planning care provision could mean that others, not you, make choices about how and where you're cared for. Denise Dent learnt a valuable lesson from her sister: 'She left it until she was no longer capable of making the decision and then it's very difficult for her son to make that choice. And I don't want to be in that position where it's the children who make the choices. If I have to go into a home I want to have identified the one I want to go into.'

However, James Dent urged against making a move into care too soon: 'You start quietening down, filling in holes and protecting and you'll find you're glad you did because that's how you are. It seems to me that going into care too early could become a self-fulfilling prophecy. So don't rush it!'

The last thing I am advocating is going into care before it's really necessary, or becoming old before your time. Heaven forbid that we should all end up like Joan Jarvis's friends: 'Cora and Stan had all the plugs in their house moved to waist height to prepare for their old age and they were about 45 at the time! They were all put that high so that they wouldn't have to bend and I thought; well that's why they've got such big stomachs because they never bend, it would do them good to bend!'

No, I'm certainly not advocating that! But what I am advocating is thinking about the possibility of needing some form of paid care in later old age and making financial provision for that care.

The above is just an overview of the issues which those considering care will need to address, and further research will be necessary. The following are some excellent websites to visit if you are interested in finding out more about long-term care.

Useful websites

Better Caring	www.bettercaring.co.uk
Elderly Accommodation Counsel	www.eac.org.uk
Office of the Public Guardian	www.guardianship.gov.uk
Commission for Social Care Inspection	www.csci.org.uk
Age Concern	www.ace.org.uk
Department of Health	ww.dh.gov.uk

5

Financial planning for retirement

'All the positive things I say about old age and retirement are based on the fact that I have money. When I say I plan treats, do this, do that, go up to London and buy something, that is all based on money. And the only thing that isn't allied to money is coming to terms with my own company. But even that is made easier by money because I can actually go out and do anything I want to do!'

Wanda Purcell

Retirement works better if you have money

Retirement works better if you have money, it's as simple as that. Greg Eaton: 'I have no fears or concerns about retirement, I think it's brilliant. There are so many things we can do. But I suppose being financially secure, as we are, makes all the difference' – you bet it does!

Our educational system is geared to preparing us for a job that will provide financially for our families; we rarely get the opportunity in our working lives to pursue a passion. Our working lives are about finding security, not about finding ourselves. There are many people working in demanding jobs just waiting for retirement and the opportunity to pursue those passionate interests. The good news is that most of us will have the time, the energy and the health in our retirement to pursue those interests; the only thing that might be missing is the money.

And what's the alternative to making financial provision for your retirement – being poor? As Colin Matthews says: 'There's nothing like poverty for bringing you down mentally and spiritually, wondering where the next penny's coming from. I've never had that worry so I'm very lucky.'

Or relying on the State? Vicky Alder:

> This country encourages you to feel secure and looked after; you've got the National Health, you've got the State pension, you've all sorts of things that comfort you and tuck you into a nice little corner and you think you're there for life. People are just not prepared for the reality of the situation. And if you haven't thought about your pension and planning for retirement you're in for a rude awakening.

So how do you make adequate financial provision for your retirement? Well, first of all you work out how much money you're going to need in retirement, you then work out how much you've already got, determine what the shortfall is and start saving.

None of this is easy stuff but doing the sums may give you an opportunity to make good any shortfalls and may ultimately lead to a feeling of comfort that you have made the best possible provision for your retirement. And it need not necessarily be rocket science. Gary Knight has taken a very practical approach: 'The only specific financial planning we've done is capital accumulation. I haven't felt the need to turn my mind to where the pennies are coming from to fund our retirement income. My logic, simple as it may be, is if we have a big enough sum to start with we'll be OK.'

HOW MUCH IS ENOUGH?

The number one worry of those people I interviewed was that they might run out of money before they died. As Sam Jarvis says: 'I suppose we've got to the stage where we can say we're not going to live for another 30 years or 20 years, maybe we'll live another 15 years and can think we've probably got enough, but have we? You don't want to see it all disappearing and you don't want to suddenly not have enough.'

How much you need in retirement isn't just about how much you want to spend in the first year or two, it's about how much you will spend over your entire retirement life. At some stage you may want to assume that spending decreases, perhaps as you get older and are less able to travel. Then towards the end of your retirement life long-term care fees may increase your spending.

When calculating how much money you are going to need in retirement you are dealing with several unknown variables: how long will you live, how much will you spend, what will inflation, interest rates, stock markets and governments do during that time?

How long will you live?

Longevity tables will tell you how long the average person of your age will live. You should know your own family history so should know whether you are genetically programmed for a long life. And you know your own current state of health, but who can predict with any accuracy how long they will live? As Mary Hardy from the department of statistics and actuarial science at the University of Waterloo in Canada says: 'The trouble with longevity is that it is a non-diversifiable risk. There really is no hedge.'

But getting this calculation wrong can have catastrophic results, as Sean Jeffries so eloquently points out:

> You need to think, well, how long am I reasonably going to live for and is the money going to run out? So you've got to assume that you are going to live for a long time because, obviously, the alternative is to say 'I'll have to go and snuff it in 10 years' time'. If you fail to snuff it at the required time you've got a big problem because you've used up all your money and you are now probably in your early dotage and there's bugger all you can do about it.

In our financial plans we assume that our clients are going to live to 99, but with the increase in the number of people living to well over 100 I have a feeling that we might be revising that figure upwards very soon.

How much will you spend?

Michelle Stansfield argues that it is difficult to know how much you'll spend in retirement until you actually get there: 'Trying to work out what you need before you retire is very hard. I assumed I'd need a lot less, and in some respects I do, but in some respects I don't because I'm going on far more holidays. But one thing's for sure – I don't want to find that I can't heat my house because the price of gas has gone up.

I think that's the worrying thing for pensioners on a fixed income because there's nowhere for them to go.'

On the other hand, pre-retiree Mary Edwards is currently keeping a detailed tally of her expenditure: 'I'm keeping a record of every single penny we spend this year and it's driving me nuts! But I want a real understanding of how much we're spending. It's preparation for retirement because I've got this rough idea in my mind of what we spend but I don't really know. It's been very valuable, the wine bill is just…, and hairdressing! Well, I mean, you've got to start with the essentials.'

Be realistic about your potential expenditure in retirement; who says you will spend less? You won't have the cost of keeping yourself in work but you might travel more, pursue new interests and existing interests more intently, and you might need money for capital projects such as starting your own business. If you're not spending your time earning, you have more time to spend spending. You might find it useful to carry out a detailed expenditure analysis like Mary Edwards, as it will at least tell you how you are currently spending your money.

Make some assumptions about the potential cost of long-term care – see Chapter 4. You might be lucky and never need paid care but it is wise to assume that you will and make the relevant provision. And remember that many costs incurred in later old age rise at a greater rate than the acknowledged rate of inflation, for example residential and nursing home fees.

And don't forget your liabilities. Remember to include repaying the mortgage or other loans.

Most of the post-retirees I interviewed were spending more money in retirement than originally planned. William Kennett: 'We tend, slightly, to live beyond our means because we are determined to enjoy the years we've got left together. My pension is enormously helpful. What amazes me is that we manage to spend it all. We spend it because we want to live and we want to do and we want to have, for example, that better bottle of wine.'

What will inflation, interest rates, stock markets, governments do?

Well, I'm of the same opinion as the anonymous person who said: 'An economic forecaster is like a cross-eyed javelin thrower: they don't win any accuracy contests, but they keep the crowd's attention.' However, in order to determine how much money you need in retirement you do have to make forecasts about the above issues. You need to estimate the future returns you might expect on your investments, both before and after retirement, and make an assumption about inflation. To the end of 2007 the annualized long-term real returns, that's the return after taking account of inflation, over the last 50 years was 7.2 per cent on equities, 2.4 per cent on gilts and 2.0 per cent on cash. The 20-year figures were 6.7 per cent on equities, 5.1 per cent on gilts and 3.5 per cent on cash (Barclays Equity and Gilt Study 2008). Do remember that these returns are gross ie before tax and charges. You probably have your own ideas about what assumptions you would like to use but it is worth remembering that many investment experts believe that returns over the next 20 years will be lower than those over the last 20 years.

Don't forget to take account of inflation in your calculations. Even a modest amount of inflation can eat into the return on your money. And while inflation rates are comparatively low at the moment, there is no guarantee that they will stay that way. Those of us who have lived through a period of high inflation will remember the toll it can take on our spending power. Maddy Lister was only 35 when her husband died, leaving her with four small children: 'He had a lot of life insurance so I was quite well provided for. But with the ensuing problems of the 1970s, with inflation at 25 per cent at one stage, the money soon ran out and I had to go out to work.'

I am not suggesting that we will have a return to those days of high inflation, but think about what inflation rate you want to assume in your calculations. See the section in Chapter 7, Investing, on the 11 deadly sins of investing under 'Forgetting about inflation'.

What about other variables?

You might want to make assumptions about downsizing your home at some stage, selling a second home, receiving an inheritance etc. But these things are harder to generalize about and are more dependent on personal situations and preferences.

One of the variables you need to take account of is when you will retire. You may be aiming at a specific date when you will stop work entirely or you may be intending to retire gradually so that you will continue to earn a reduced income for a period of time. Of course, you may find that your plans are thwarted if some of the assumptions you use in your planning turn out to be inaccurate. Carl Armstrong, our self-titled Mr Misery, had his own comment on what might happen to throw the planning figures out of kilter: 'Again Mr Misery says sometimes the economy is just going to be bad. If that happened between now and our planned retirement date we might have to keep on working for longer. So our retirement age might be determined either by our choice or by economic circumstances.' OK, so if the worst happens you might have to keep on working a bit longer, but it's better to try to hit a target and miss slightly than to have no target at all.

HOW MUCH HAVE YOU GOT?

So, you've done the sums and you know how much you would like to spend each year when you are retired. You've also identified the liabilities you would like to repay and any potential future costs, over and above daily spending. Now you need to find out how much you've already got, for example investments, pensions, savings etc. You will need to estimate what they will be worth when you retire – what spending power they will give you. Once you've done that, you can calculate the shortfall between what you will have and what you need. When you know what the shortfall is you can draw up a savings plan to make up the deficit.

It should be easy, but when you retire your income will come from several sources, including: State pension, occupational pension, personal pensions, investment and savings income, income from rental property, sale of a property or business, continuing to work and earn an income, inheritances. This means that you will need to find out what several things are worth now, what they might be worth in the future and what income they are likely to provide you with when you retire.

What are your pensions worth?

According to the Pension Commission, we have the most complex pensions system in the world. And in deference to this there is a separate chapter – Chapter 9 – that covers pensions and gives information about how to find out what your current pensions are worth, how to increase your pension and what's the best way to take benefits from your pension.

What are your investments worth?

Investments come in various shapes and sizes, but they all count towards your retirement savings pot. You may have a very simple investment portfolio comprising cash in a building society or in a sock under the mattress. Or you might have a very complicated investment portfolio with equities, ISAs, gilts, corporate bonds, National Savings, private equity, property etc.

Whatever is in your portfolio, you will need to make assumptions about what it might be worth when you retire. To do this you need to decide the potential rate of growth of the investments. You might be happy to lump (technical term) all your investments together and apply one growth rate to the whole lot. This is the pragmatic approach but you do need to be a pragmatist to apply it; obviously, if the majority of the portfolio is in cash you won't be applying a potential annualized rate of return of 10 per cent!

Alternatively, you could break the portfolio down into its constituent parts and apply a separate growth rate to each part. The Barclays Equity and Gilt study figures for long-term returns on equities, gilts and cash are listed above but you will probably have your own views on what returns you want to apply. And remember, as already mentioned, many investment experts believe that returns over the next 20 years will be lower than those over the last 20 years.

And, I know I keep saying this, but don't forget to account for the tax you may be liable to pay on investment returns and the cost of the investments themselves.

The major aim of this part of the exercise is to identify where your money is at the moment and try to determine if it will be enough to give you the retirement life you want. And if it isn't enough, devise a strategy for saving more.

Does the value of your home count?

It is possible to use the equity in your home to help fund the cost of living in retirement. I am often asked about this subject and have included a separate chapter – Chapter 8 – that deals with it. However, using your home to generate extra money is something that needs careful consideration. Don't assume that your home is your pension based on house price rises over the past two decades; this is a critical error because increases in property values will not continue indefinitely, as recent history has shown.

Accounting for the value of second properties

If you have a second property that you let out, or indeed a third, fourth and so on, the income they generate, after costs and tax, will subsidize your retirement income. You will need to make assumptions about that rental income; what it might increase (or decrease!) by each year, periods of non-occupancy etc. You might also want to make assumptions about selling the property, or properties, as you get older to inject capital into your portfolio. Again you will need to make assumptions about capital returns on property, remembering that you might be liable for capital gains tax on any sales of properties that are not your principal residence.

You may have investment in commercial property and will need to take net rent and a possible future sale into account.

If you have a second property that is a holiday home you might want to factor in the sale of the property at some time in the future and use of the money generated to help fund your retirement. Holiday homes may be fine while you're comparatively fit and able to travel, but as you get older it may become more of a chore to keep and visit a second property. But don't forget that the sale of a second property may result in a capital gains tax charge.

What might your business interests be worth?

Nowhere is planning in advance for retirement more important than when you are running your own business. Not only do you have to plan your retirement but you also have to plan how you will make a successful exit from the business, both practically and financially. If your retirement depends on being able to sell your business, make sure you plan well in advance for its disposal or passing on; talk to experts and get a valuation so you know what it's worth. An expert will help you explore all the possibilities open to you, but don't leave it until the last minute because planning and preparing a business for sale can take years.

If you have a business interest, private or partnership, you will have to make some assumptions about the sale value of that interest. It may be that a prescribed formula is applied when someone leaves the organization and their interest is being bought out, or it may just be that you sell it for whatever someone is prepared to pay for it. Going through the exercise of identifying what the potential shortfall is between your existing provision and what you need to fund your retirement is excellent for making you focus on how much you need to sell a business interest for to make good that shortfall.

Should you include possible inheritances?

My advice is not to bank on receiving any inheritances. People change their minds about who they are going to leave their money to. And potential inheritances can get eaten up paying for care home fees for those who were going to leave you the money. Plan as if you weren't going to receive any inheritances and then if they come your way they're a bonus.

There may be occasions when you feel justified in using a potential inheritance in your planning, but be honest with yourself about the chances of it going wrong.

Don't forget to include possible future employment income

Modern-day retirement isn't necessarily about stopping work, so you might want to include a degree of continuing income on the plus side of the spreadsheet. HSBC's recent survey, *The Future of Retirement: What the World Wants*, found that people's attitude to working in retirement is changing. Of those interviewed for the survey in the UK, 10 per cent want to continue working full time in retirement, 20 per cent never want to work again and 70 per cent want to continue working but on a flexible basis.

When they were asked why they wanted to continue working in retirement, only 24 per cent said for the money. The responses from the other 76 per cent ranged from: for mental stimulation, to keep physically active, to have something meaningful to do or to connect with others.

Employers are being encouraged to acknowledge that older workers have a lot to offer. And the tightening of the labour supply as a result of decreasing birth rates is already beginning to make older workers look more attractive to employers.

But be realistic about how much you might earn in retirement. While you worked you might have risen to a position that commanded a high salary, but the flexible work you choose to do in retirement might not generate the same level of income. Dr Ken Dychtwald, Special Adviser on Global Ageing to HSBC: 'Employers have already begun to change their opinions of older people in the workforce, but employees need to meet them halfway. Crucially, they need to remain flexible – being open to new ways of working and to drawing a salary according to merit rather than tenure.'

So, no assuming that you will be earning £100,000 per annum from that part-time job unless you really do merit it.

And, finally, remember to deduct liabilities

Don't forget to assess your potential liabilities and include those on the withdrawal side of the equation. The chances are that if you have a mortgage or other borrowing you will want to pay these off before going into retirement. There are occasions when having a debt against your estate can be beneficial in saving inheritance tax, but you need to be careful that you are not depriving yourself of income and that the borrowing isn't costly debt.

It's a balance!

In all this planning I think it is important to remember that it is a balance between saving for the future but living in, and enjoying, the moment. Maggie Armstrong recognizes that she and Carl are currently able to put money aside for retirement savings but she doesn't want to do this at the cost of having a bit of fun now: 'I think at this stage we are probably at our maximum earning potential. And we're trying to strike a balance between enjoying some of the rewards of our labours now, but also trying to maximize savings so that when we do finally retire there is enough in the pot to manage.'

WHAT'S NEXT?

Hopefully the above has helped you to make some assumptions about your longevity, spending rate, investment returns, the current size of your retirement savings and any other variables unique to you. That was the easy bit – now you need to bring that all together into some form of lifelong cash flow planner.

How can a lifelong cash flow planner help – and what is it anyway?

A lifelong cash flow planner is a spreadsheet into which you feed all the data you've gathered and assumptions you've made. On one side you have what you are starting with – the 'how much have you got' plus future incomings such as earnings, pensions etc. This side also includes any other future incomings such as selling a second home or downsizing your main home. On the other side you enter what you're going to spend between now and when you die, including repaying liabilities such as a mortgage. All this is calculated to the date we are assuming you'll die, using the growth and inflation figures you are comfortable with.

A lifelong cash flow planner will show you the shortfall, or surplus, in the financial provision you have made for your future and, armed with this knowledge, you can then decide what to do about it. It might be that you cannot afford to make any more money available for savings, so you might have to think about trimming your future expenditure. The really great thing about a lifelong cash flow planner is that you can play 'what if'. For example: 'What if I retired at 55 instead of 60?' or 'What if we bought a second home in two years' time?' or 'What if I gave my daughter £50,000 to help her buy a house?' or anything else that you might like to think about doing. The cash flow planner will tell you the financial implications of those actions and you can make sensible choices about the future. It might be that you could retire at 55 instead of 60 but you would have to save extra each month to do it. Or you might be able to buy that second home but you would have to wait four years not two. And you might be able to help your daughter buy a house but you could only afford to give her £30,000.

A criticism of cash flow planning is that the assumptions used may turn out to be incorrect. I always say to clients that every assumption we use will be wrong. But I use the analogy of a journey across the States from San Diego to New York – we aren't trying to get there to the very second, we are just trying to get there on the right day.

In any event, financial planning isn't a destination – it's a journey. You need to keep reviewing your financial plan because, as sure as eggs are eggs, things will change and regular reviews help to keep you on track.

This is what Mary Edwards had to say about the benefit of lifelong cash flow planning: 'The cash flow projections have been remarkably helpful in reassuring us about where we will be when our salaries drop by half, or when we go down to just pension and so on. It's confirmed that what we want to spend on holidays etc going forward is reasonable. And it's helped us identify when we might have to sell our overseas property and when we might have to downsize.'

There is proprietary software available to help you build a lifelong cash flow planner, or you might want to construct your own spread-sheet. This is what Sean Jeffries did:

> I tried my hand at building a spreadsheet. I kept it simple and just said – look, how much do I think that I reasonably need to spend each year, what is the likely rate of return and inflation, and how much money is

there in the kitty and what happens when it runs out. Once I'd talked with my financial planner and had been told that I wasn't doing anything stupid in the calculations it gave me comfort. It also gave me confidence to sell my part of the business because I knew what I had to sell it for to make the figures balance!

Knowing what the shortfall in your planning is can be very helpful when you are negotiating the sale of anything going into retirement.

But ideally you should be working with a financial planner. Even Sean Jeffries with his spreadsheet skills felt more comfortable with the results of his endeavours after his planner had checked it out for him. At the end of this chapter is a section on finding and working with a financial planner.

What if you don't want to use a financial planner and don't know one end of a spreadsheet from another?

Do you need to work with a financial planner to ensure you have a financially independent retirement? Do you need to construct a life-long cash flow planner to make sure that you don't die broke? Of course not! A lot of people make very good financial provision for their retirement without even looking at a spreadsheet.

This is Amy Pillinger's view: 'I've never done any projections, the sort of thing that tells me that if I'm spending at this rate, and accruing interest on my money at this rate, my money will go on for so long. I'm afraid I have a fairly casual approach to such matters.' Casual maybe but nonetheless canny, Amy has always been a careful budgeter. And her partner, Colin Matthews, adds: 'All through life I think we had a Micawber approach to financial planning, we never ever kept accounts, I just look to see that money coming in should be equal to, or be slightly more than, money going out each month.'

The most important thing to realize is that the period spent in retirement is likely to be a long one, a healthy one and has the potential to be a happy one. But it is likely to be more fulfilling if you have made adequate financial provision – I don't know of any situation where having money has made it worse. Nearly everyone I interviewed said that being able to do what they wanted to do, when they wanted to do it, was the number one thing they were looking forward to in retirement. And as Barry Rudd says: 'What allows you to do what you want to do when you want to do it? Financial independence allows you to do that.' So, get saving!

HOW TO GET MORE OF IT

Once you've identified the potential shortfall between the amount of money you're likely to need in retirement and the provision you've already made, you can devise a savings programme.

Saving more for retirement isn't just about stuffing more money into your pension fund; that might be part of it but it is unlikely to be the whole. Saving for retirement is about saving into a diverse range of investments. You'll find tips on saving more in Chapter 9 on pensions and Chapter 7 on investing.

Most people leave planning for retirement too late and have to play catch-up and this will influence the risk they are prepared to take with their investments and therefore the return on those investments. Sometimes family circumstances mean that it's not possible to save early on. Brad Isles: 'We're fortunate in that in the last 10 years we've had money to invest. But it has only been in the last 10 years, not long enough really. We've taken a path through life, we've had divorces, we were both broke when we got together 16 years ago and this is what we're left with now, and we'll make the most of it. I just feel that we kind of want a lot more but this is it for now.'

And I'll let Maddy Lister have the final word of advice about making sure you've got enough income in retirement: 'It's very important, when you please yourself and live the life you want, doing the things you want to do, that you've got an income to support it.'

WHAT ARE THE ADVANTAGES OF WORKING WITH A FINANCIAL PLANNER?

A financial 'planner' will help you to take an objective view of your present situation and help you plan and achieve the goals you have set yourself. This approach is different to that offered by a financial 'adviser' who will focus on product sales. A financial planner will focus on your needs first before recommending a course of action. Most planners have been trained to take a broad look at your financial situation, while other professionals may focus on a particular area of your financial life.

Goal setting is an integral part of the financial planning process, on the basis that you are far more likely to hit a target if you know what you are aiming at than if you are firing blindly into space. Goals in retirement might be different from those you set yourself in pre-retirement when you were concentrating on accumulating assets, paying off the mortgage and educating your children. Retirement goals are about identifying what you want to do with the rest of your life, and what you need to do to achieve them.

Barry Rudd has worked with his financial planner since his early 30s:

> Financial planning just struck a chord with me. I thought this is the way of helping us define and achieve what we wanted to do. It just seemed a very useful tool for my approach to controlling my own destiny. There's a discipline in making sure that you understand where the money is and what's happening to it. Financial planning gives you the confidence that at some point, not too distant, you'll be financially independent.

A financial planner will also help you make decisions about how to invest your money in a way that you are comfortable with. Anita Rudd: 'I think it took away a lot of the worry about wondering whether we had made the best decisions for our money. Left to my own devices I would have stuffed it all in a building society. So for me, having that professional overview that could recommend, suggest and give us some guidance without actually telling us what to do was very helpful.'

What is financial planning?

Financial planning is the process of meeting your life goals through the proper management of your finances. The financial planning process helps you take a 'big picture' look at where you are now, where you want to go and what you need to do to get there. A good analogy is a long road trip; you wouldn't dream of setting off without looking at a map and planning your route or entering your destination in your satnav! A financial planner will work with you, helping you to pinpoint where you are now on the map of life, your place 'A', and where you want to be, your place 'B'. The planner will then agree with you a route for the journey and an estimated time of arrival; having done that they will help you stick to the route because life is like any other journey, you can take a wrong turning when something unexpected happens. This big picture approach to your financial goals sets a financial planner apart from other financial advisers who may have been trained to focus on a particular area of your financial life.

What if you don't know what your life goals are?

What if you don't know your place 'B' on the map of life? What if you're working so hard you haven't had time even to think what your life in retirement might look like? A good financial planner should be able to work with you so that you are able to identify and articulate goals. Alternatively, or as well as, you might want to consider working with a life coach.

The following chapter, entitled 'Life coaching – there are no career counsellors for the over-55s!', explores the value that life coaches can add to those people approaching or in the early stages of retirement.

Can you be your own financial planner?

Of course you can and many people do it very successfully. There is certainly no lack of information available to everyone out there, but this is another paradox of modern life – the more information there is the harder it is to choose wisely among all the financial noise and hype. I am a keen advocate for using a planner in the following circumstances:

- You need expertise you don't possess, eg tax planning advice, risk evaluation.
- You want to get a professional opinion about the financial plan you've developed for yourself.
- You might have the ability but you have neither the time nor the inclination to do your own financial planning.
- You have an immediate and unexpected life event eg inheritance, major illness.
- You feel that a professional planner could provide an objective overview of how you currently manage your finances.

How do you choose a good financial planner?

One problem is that anyone can call themselves a financial planner, so you need to have your wits about you when selecting a planner. Ask friends and colleagues if they use a planner and if they can recommend them to you. Often a personal recommendation is the best way to find a good financial planner.

The Institute of Financial Planning is the professional body for financial planners. Its website is www.financialplanning.org and you can search for a certified financial planner under geographical areas as well as specialisms. There is a profile for each of the planners on the website.

The Personal Finance Society is the financial planning arm of the Chartered Insurance Institute and is its professional body for financial planners and advisers. Its website is www.thepfs.org. Here you can search for a chartered financial planner. Both websites have excellent tips on how to find a good planner.

It is always sensible to see at least three potential planners so that you get a feel for the services they provide and can choose a planner that you feel entirely comfortable and compatible with. The following list of questions to ask a planner should help you choose the best person for you. While many of the questions can be asked over the telephone or by e-mail, and you might want to do this to narrow down the field, I strongly recommend face-to-face meetings with potential planners so that you can really assess them:

Ten questions to ask when choosing a financial planner

1. **What experience do they have?** How long has the planner been in practice, what work experience do they have? Is their experience compatible with the work you want them to do?
2. **What are their qualifications?** Look for a planner who is either a Certified Financial Planner, licensed via the Institute of Financial Planning (search for one on www.financialplanning.org) or a Chartered Financial Planner, licensed via The Personal Finance Society (search for one on www.thepfs.org). Both of these will have had to undergo a rigorous series of examinations to obtain their qualifications. If the planner holds a financial planning designation or certification, check on their background with The Financial Services Authority (FSA) at www.fsa.gov.uk.
3. **What services do they offer?** Choose a planner that offers the range of services most appropriate to your needs.
4. **What is their approach to financial planning?** Ask about the type of clients and financial situations they typically like to work with. Is your situation one that they are used to dealing with and enjoy?

    Does the planner require you to have a minimum level of capital and/or income before offering services? Do you meet the minimum requirement?
5. **Will they be the only person working with you?** The financial planner may work with you themselves or have others in the office to assist them. You may want to meet everyone who will be working with you.

6. **How will you pay for the service?** The planner should tell you clearly how they will be paid for the services provided. They should confirm this in writing. Planners are typically paid in one of two ways, either by commissions or by fees. In some cases it is possible that a combination of fees and commissions may be used. My own personal preference, and the way I work, is to be paid by a fee. In this way everyone knows exactly where they stand and I don't have to keep recommending products that generate a commission just to make sure that I get paid.

7. **Could anyone besides you benefit from their recommendations?** Does the planner have relationships or partnerships that should be disclosed to you? For instance, they may receive an introductory fee for referring you to an accountant or solicitor for implementation of planning suggestions.

8. **Have they ever been publicly disciplined for any unlawful or unethical actions in their professional career?** The FSA keeps records on the disciplinary history of financial planners. To check the disciplinary history of a financial planner, contact the Financial Services Authority, 25 The Colonade, Canary Wharf, London E14 5HS. Telephone: 020 7066 1000. Website: www.fsa.gov.uk.

9. **Can you have it in writing?** Ask the planner to provide you with a written agreement that details the services that will be provided. Keep this document for future reference.

10. **What do they expect from you?** A financial planning relationship is a two-way street. As well as you depending on your planner to deliver an excellent and effective service, your planner will depend on you. A good question to ask the planner is 'If we were sitting here in three years' time and our relationship had been a success, what would I have needed to do to help to make that relationship a success?' In turn, tell the planner exactly what they would have needed to do over that period to make the relationship a success from your point of view. In this way both the client and the planner are left in no doubt as to what each of them needs to do to make and maintain an excellent professional relationship.

Most important of all, look for a financial planner who will put you and your needs at the centre of every financial planning decision.

6

Life coaching

'It's not that we're putting off thinking about retirement. I can't actually visualize it well enough to know what I think I'm going to want to do. At the moment we are still working full time and we're working long hours.'
Maggie Armstrong

THERE ARE NO CAREER COUNSELLORS FOR THE OVER-55S!

The time you spend in retirement could last as long as the time you spend working. And while there was lots of help available to you when you first entered the job market, none of this is available on entering the third, and potentially most fulfilling, period of your life. OK, some of the big companies put on retirement-planning seminars but these are usually based around generic advice given on a group basis.

So what do you do if you feel that you are in danger of not making good use of your time in retirement, of not achieving everything you feel you could achieve? What if you want to set yourself a challenge to discover something new but are so busy setting business targets you don't know where to start on your own life targets? What if, like Nell Priest, you want: 'To break out of the rut and to see whether there are new challenges that can be met and enjoyed.'

But what if you are working so hard that you don't have time to think about what you might do in retirement? If, like Carl Armstrong, you know that: 'Retirement could be good, a huge vista that opens up.' But you just don't have enough time to explore it?

Well, you could do what a lot of transitional retirees do and spend a couple of years immediately after retirement looking for inspiration. This certainly seems to work for some. It is a period of reflection and a chance to 'smell the roses'. But suppose, after two years, inspiration doesn't strike?

You may be happy just 'to be'. You may feel that the idea of challenging yourself is for the birds. Several interviewees said that they had had a belly-full of objective setting in their jobs and didn't want to even think about such things in retirement, although these were mostly pre- and transitional retirees. And even they occasionally admitted that: 'I just feel somehow that I would want to take a look back at the week and say "I've done that this week, or I achieved that" or whatever. I feel a certain guilt if I don't challenge myself enough and I don't know why I feel guilty about that but I do' – Anita Rudd.

And then there are those people who want to continue working, or need to continue working to subsidize their pension. How do they identify what might be a fulfilling occupation?

As the title of this section says, 'there are no career counsellors for the over-55s', but there are life coaches.

Charlotte Hitchings (her real name) is a life and business coach who works with people approaching periods of change in their lives such as retirement: 'I've had clients who know they are going to go through change and they don't know what they want at the end of it.' Charlotte is used to working with people who may not have had an opportunity to identify what they want to do: 'They may not walk in saying "I know I want to do XYZ," they may come in and say "I'm going through some major change and I really need some help in exploring what will make my life more fulfilling in the future." '

I asked Charlotte how this approach worked with people nearing retirement: 'Part of the process is to explore with the person what things they always wanted to do that they've never had time to do because they've been so busy working. And what would they want to look back on in their lives and see that they had achieved, other than their work. What other aspects have not been explored in their lives that they might now be able to spend time bringing into their lives.'

So what exactly is life coaching? Charlotte: 'Life coaching is working with somebody who is completely objective, to define what you want to achieve and work out how you're going to achieve it. Your coach then continues working with you to help you actually achieve your goals or outcomes.'

Not only do life coaches have skills to help you frame a good goal so that it is going to get you really excited and committed to it, they also have questioning skills to make you look at things from a different perspective. So even if you feel clueless about what you might want to do in retirement, a life coach can help you explore who you are, your talents and motivations, until you find an aim to inspire you.

And even if you're looking forward to the change retirement will bring to your life, it can be a daunting time. A life coach like Charlotte recognizes this: 'When people are facing major change it's quite a scary and lonely time for them. Even if they know other people who are going through it as well, it's still them, as an individual on their own, facing those changes.' And a life coach will give you emotional support through the change process: 'They are completely on your side so there is emotional support. The coach is there for you, as the client. The coach only has one agenda in the relationship and that's your agenda. What you want, the coach wants you to get.'

The coaching process works differently depending on the coach you are working with and your needs. Charlotte works on a 12-stage life-coaching process: 'The 12 sessions are usually one every week or fortnight. The reason for such frequent sessions is to keep the momentum going.' Sessions usually last between one and one and a quarter hours and can be in person or on the phone. Charges for life coaching vary and you are probably looking at anything between £50 and £200 per session.

How do you find a life coach? The International Coach Federation has a website, www.coachfederation.org, where you can search for a coach. You can also search the Association for Coaching website: www.associationforcoaching.com. You can look in Yellow Pages or the adverts in the Sunday newspapers. However, it is such a personal thing that it is better to try to get a recommendation to a coach from someone you know and trust and who has used that coach.

Up until recently, life coaching was unregulated but most coaches will have been through some formal training process and have certification. This is Charlotte's advice: 'Look for a certified coach who has been through a coach-specific training course and who has, or is working towards, a professional credential through either the International Coach Federation or the Association for Coaching. There are also diplomas and even a master's degree in coaching now.' So if you are planning to use a life coach, check out their credentials and experience and make sure you feel comfortable with them on a personal level.

Life coaching isn't airy-fairy. As Charlotte explains: 'It's very outcome focused. It's interesting because it is extremely practical in the sense that it's about tangible things you build into your life. However, it's also about intangible interactions between you, your life and the people in it. I can't emphasize this enough – it isn't just about doing stuff, it's also about learning stuff about yourself and that's the really profound bit.'

Gary Knight, at the age of 48, is someway off retirement but he was not alone in realizing that the success of his retirement depends on what he decides to do with his life after work: 'I think that my motivation in retirement, and how much I enjoy retirement, will depend on the structure I manage to put into my life. I think if I can structure some things that interest me I won't have a problem.'

It stands to reason that if you make a connection at an early stage to 'What comes next?' then you are likely to be much more enthusiastic and excited about retirement than those who put off thinking about it. A life coach may be the very person you need to help you put that structure and interest into your retirement life.

USEFUL WEBSITES

The International Coach Federation   www.coachfederation.org
The Association for Coaching   www.associationforcoaching.com

7

Investing

'If it had been up to me I would have stuffed it all in a sock under the mattress and that would have been it because I would have been so anxious about where to invest it, but that wouldn't have been very sensible.'

Helen Kennett

I am not about to give you the formula for the perfect investment strategy because such a strategy does not exist. But I'll give you a formula for an effective investment strategy: **Just start saving.**

Don't be put off saving because you're worried about the stock market or about being ripped off by an unscrupulous adviser. Be sensible, do your homework and just do it.

Investors are always looking for Utopia; an investment that is risk free, provides a high level of income, is instantly accessible and gives a good capital return after inflation and tax have taken their toll. It is not possible to have all this in one investment, but a mixture of different investments, which is what a well-balanced portfolio should be, will go some way towards providing it.

Your investment strategy for retirement will depend on how far away retirement is for you – the longer the better, obviously. There is the potential to take more risks with your investments if you are looking long term. Riskier investments, such as equities, can go up and down in value like a yo-yo in the short term so are not good investments if you need your money back soon, say within five years. But such investments have, historically, produced better returns over the longer term compared with cash and deposit-type investments, so they are good if you don't need your money back soon and you're prepared to take some risk.

Your strategy might also depend on what you need the money for. For example, you might know that you will need to buy a new car in three years' time and don't want to take the risk of not having the money available to pay for it. So you might decide to save and keep the 'car money' in a cash account. But for another purchase, say a boat in 15 years' time, you might be prepared to take more risk with your investment strategy, knowing that you have time to weather the ups and downs of equity-type investments. I refer to this approach to investing as 'event investing'. It's how they used to save in years gone by. Then they had different 'pots' for putting their money in to meet different needs: the 'rent money pot', the 'food money pot', the 'holiday money pot' etc. Thank goodness most of us are financially more fortunate than those past generations, but the principle still holds good. Also, making sure that the money for your short-term needs and necessities is secure enables you to be a bit more adventurous when investing spare money for your longer-term needs – such as retirement!

If retirement is imminent the most pressing investment issue you will be faced with is moving from the accumulation phase of investment to the consuming phase. The accumulation phase is when you are saving to get enough money into pensions and investments to feather your retirement nest. The consuming phase is when you are trying to take income and capital, as efficiently as you possibly can, from your portfolio to fund your retirement lifestyle without depleting your reserves too soon.

It isn't easy. First of all, it is difficult to determine how much is enough – see Chapter 5 – Financial planning for retirement. For example, £1m might look a lot but what sort of income can you expect from it? If you assume a 4 per cent pre-tax return, that's £40,000 gross per annum. That might or might not be enough. Why 4 per cent? Is that a figure I've just plucked out of thin air? No, it's a figure I tend to work to when advising clients. Using a return of 4 per cent gross is the average, long-term return you can expect from a well-balanced portfolio that is maintaining its ability to grow in capital value and provide you with an income that keeps pace with inflation. Perhaps 4 per cent errs on the side of caution, but I like to take into account the fact that most post-retirees tend to have a more cautious attitude to risk.

You may also need to factor into your sums capital consumption. Your savings may not be enough to enable you to live off the income they generate and you may need to gradually withdraw some of the capital to subsidize your living expenses. If you are depleting capital in this way you are also likely to be depleting the regular income from that capital, simply because the capital sum generating the income keeps getting smaller. Careful planning is necessary here to make sure that your capital doesn't expire before you do!

Also, moving from the accumulation phase to the consuming phase can bring problems. People are likely to acquire the habit of saving during the accumulation phase, and this is a difficult habit to break. As an adviser I find that I have more trouble persuading my retired clients to spend their money than I do persuading them to tighten their purse strings, although during the transition from accumulation to consuming it is important to recognize the spending limitations imposed when income drops.

Portfolio management can become more complex during the consuming phase. When you are in retirement you are managing money to provide capital for retirement projects, income for living, savings to pay for potential long-term care fees and non-emergency medical treatment, something to leave to your heirs and probably no new money coming into the portfolio. And not knowing how long it all has to last or what inflation, interest rates and the markets will do. All this needs regular reviewing and careful managing. The conventional view is that it is the accumulation phase of investing that needs close attention – well, it does, but perhaps the consuming phase needs even closer attention.

ELEVEN DEADLY SINS OF INVESTING

What follows are the 11 deadly sins of investing – mistakes that I've seen people make time and time again. By avoiding these deadly sins you are well on the way to making a success of your investment strategy.

1. Not having a diverse portfolio

Money is like manure – if you pile it up in one corner it smells, if you spread it around it helps things to grow. No one knows what is going to be the next big investment 'thing'. In the late 1990s it was technology. More recently it has been property. Asset classes, and individual elements within those asset classes, come in and out of favour on a cyclical basis. Accept that you don't know which of your investments is going to earn you the best return over the next 10 years, but look forward to finding out because you have an exposure to more than one asset class. Also accept that if you have a diverse portfolio you are likely to have at least one investment that is in the doldrums, but that might be the very investment that in five years' time is riding the crest of the wave.

However, don't over-diversify, because that can be just as counter-productive. If you have £100,000 to invest I would not recommend putting £2,000 into each of 50 funds, for example. That is expensive because you don't get the reduction in costs that investment companies sometimes give if larger sums are invested. It is also an administration and monitoring nightmare! And there is no guarantee that you are gaining greater diversification – the chances are that you are unwittingly duplicating investment exposure. And I am not saying that you should hold every single asset class in your portfolio in the name of diversity when it is quite obvious that one or more asset classes are over-valued.

2. Saving without a purpose

Have a plan for your savings and stick to it; whether it's paying off your mortgage, helping your children or boosting your retirement savings. Different investment needs tend to have different time horizons, so consider using different investments; cash or cash equivalent for short-term needs, say, but for longer-term needs other investments eg equity/property/commodities etc.

3. Trying to time the market

It is impossible to time the stock market. Investment is not a science; if it were we would all be rich – or poor probably because there would be no uncertainty. Uncertainty brings opportunity and opportunity can bring profit, but it can bring loss. Don't try to time the market. If you, or you and your adviser, think that a particular investment is right for you, invest. It is natural to worry that the stock market will drop just after you've invested, and it might, but if you are in equity investments you should be thinking long term and be prepared to ride out short-term fluctuations in the market.

Alternatively, a good solution is to invest smaller amounts on a regular basis as this reduces the risk of suffering a big loss just after investing.

4. Chasing performance

While we are told that past performance is no guarantee of future results, there is a tendency to look back and see how an investment fund has performed historically. If you are going to do this, and it is tempting because what else do you have to go on, be careful. Make sure that the statistics you are looking at are giving you a complete and accurate picture.

Investors have a tendency to invest in assets or funds that performed best over the last three years, but this can be investment suicide. Think logically: if an investment has performed well for three years the chances are that it's become expensive and if you pay a lot for an asset you can expect lower returns in the future. This is borne out time after time throughout history – just think of the technology boom and bust in the late 1990s/early 2000.

There is a mountain of academic evidence showing that active managers fail to consistently outperform the market over the long term. This shouldn't come as a surprise because active managers make up the bulk of the market and, by the simple rules of arithmetic, the average manager will simply provide the return of the market less costs. The key problem is that those costs are very high indeed, which brings me on to my next deadly sin…

5. Not taking account of charges

It is important to be aware of the charges you will pay to the investment companies when you invest. Costs are very important. Several economic commentators believe that returns from investments are likely to be lower in the future. Say the return on the equity portion of your portfolio is 8 per cent per annum, and you are paying 2 per cent each year to the investment companies in charges, then that is reducing your return by 25 per cent.

To lower the cost of investing and potentially increase your return, it might be worth looking at passive funds such as index trackers. Passive funds try to capture the return that the market is delivering as cheaply as possible, and this is a sensible investment approach. If you can capture market return at a cost of 0.2 per cent per annum via a passive fund then you are doing so 10 times cheaper than through an actively managed fund.

6. Trusting your future to cash

Bank and building society deposit accounts are an ideal place to keep money for short-term investment needs: a new car, a holiday etc. They are also an excellent home for an 'emergency fund', a sum of rainy day money put on one side to be used for those unforeseen needs. And on this issue it is always wise to build up a cash emergency fund to cover, say, six months' expenditure – just in case – before you embark on a more diversified savings programme. Bank and building society deposit accounts are usually very secure and you know that your money will be there when you need it. But this security comes at a price, and that price is lower returns than you can expect on most other asset classes over the longer term. The problem is that, over time, even modest levels of inflation eat into the value of the after-tax return on cash.

7. Missing out on tax breaks

It's the after-tax return that matters. Don't just focus on the gross return on your investments – look at the net, after tax, return that you receive; after all, this is the money that you will have in your wallet to spend. The tax efficiency of your portfolio can make a big difference to the spendable return.

First of all, make sure that you use your tax allowances. If you are a married couple and happy to take the approach of 'what's mine is yours', make sure that investments are shared between you in such a way that each of you is receiving income to set against your personal income tax allowance.

If one of you is a higher-rate taxpayer and one of you is a basic-rate taxpayer, can you re-jig your investments so that the basic-rate taxpayer receives more investment income and the higher-rate taxpayer less?

Each year you have a capital gains tax allowance that means you can sell assets that incur a capital gain, up to a certain level, without having to pay tax. By doing this you are taking money, tax free, from investments that are growing in capital value; an excellent way of providing additional 'income' in a very tax-efficient manner.

Invest in tax-efficient investments: ISAs, pensions, some National Savings and Investments offerings, gilts, or, at the riskier end of the investment spectrum, Enterprise Investment Schemes and Venture Capital Trusts. Talk to your planner about which ones would be appropriate for you.

8. Taking risks you are not comfortable with or don't understand

I always remember a client saying to me: 'It's not the return on my money that I worry about, it's the return of my money.' Some people are so risk averse that they just do not want to take any risk with their money whatsoever, while others are prepared to take a high degree of risk.

Risk means different things to different people but there is no such thing as a risk-free investment. If you keep your money in a sock under the mattress, the risk is it could be stolen, eaten or burnt. Keep it in a cash account and the risk is that the purchasing power of your money will be eroded over time by inflation. Invest in other asset classes, from fixed interest through property to equities, and the risk is that the capital value of your money could go down.

The important thing is that you know what risk you are taking with your investment portfolio. All too often I see people who have no idea of the level of risk they are exposed to via their investments. Part of the problem is that we allow this four-letter word 'risk' to float around the room without actually pinning it to the wall and analysing exactly what it means to you.

You may be quite happy to carry out your own risk assessment and identify that the level of risk you are taking with your investments is one that you are happy to take. However, a good financial planner will analyse your risk profile in both an objective and subjective way. Subjectively your planner should be able to gain a good knowledge of your appetite for risk from the face-to-face discussions you've had together.

There are several risk assessment tools on the market that help your planner to carry out an objective risk analysis, usually via a series of sophisticated questionnaires. Don't balk at this, because the results can be very illuminating, often throwing up contradictions in the investor's philosophy, for example wanting a 10 per cent return from the portfolio but not wanting to expose any investments to the risk of capital loss! Such contradictions are an opportunity for the planner and investor to have a 'reality check' discussion and education.

Most importantly, the results of the risk analysis will form the basis of your portfolio model and will help your adviser plan a portfolio that is within your risk tolerances while endeavouring to provide the level of return you are looking for.

One final point on risk – don't take more risk than you need to. If you only need a low rate of return from your investments to secure your financial future – why take more risks to achieve a greater return?

9. Failing to review your investments

Over time, legislation will change, taxation will change, the economic situation will change, markets will change and you and your situation will change. It is important to review your investments regularly to make sure that you are still on track to achieve your financial objectives.

It is also a good discipline to rebalance your portfolio on a regular basis, taking into account, of course, the potential cost of any rebalancing. Your investment strategy has probably followed a model: an approach either you, or you and your adviser, have devised to ensure that your investments are spread between a number of assets – cash, fixed interest, equities etc. Over time, certain assets will have performed better than others and the portfolio will have become unbalanced. Does this matter? Well, yes it does, because the unbalanced portfolio may no longer reflect your risk profile or be on line to deliver the returns you are looking for. It is human nature to hang on to the investments that are performing well and sell those that aren't, but this isn't always wise and a rebalancing strategy makes you review this approach. By selling a portion of the investments that are performing well you bring the portfolio back in line with the agreed model. If you are able to do this using your capital gains tax allowance then it is a very tax-efficient way of rebalancing or realizing proceeds from the portfolio. The realized proceeds can then be reinvested back into the portfolio, in line with the agreed model, or spent or gifted away.

10. Forgetting about inflation

A high rate of inflation can be dangerous because over time it can eat into the return from your investments and/or income and consequently into your purchasing power. For example, if inflation is running at 3.0 per cent per annum, your income, or return from your investments, has to deliver an after-tax and after-costs growth of 3.0 per cent per annum just to keep your purchasing power at its current level. This is why it is important to measure the 'real rate of return' on your investments. The real rate of return is the return after taking account of inflation. If inflation is running at 3 per cent and your investments are delivering a return of 4 per cent, you are achieving a real rate of return of 1 per cent. It is worth remembering that not all inflation is bad; a modest rate of inflation is a result of sustainable economic growth so is a good sign and puts me in mind of the saying 'Inflation is like sin, every government denounces it but they all practise it.'

How is inflation measured? Well, since 2003 the government has used a statistical measure of inflation known as CPI (consumer price index). The CPI is calculated according to a basket of goods and services that the Office of National Statistics judges to be representative of the way in which the typical person in Britain spends their money. But CPI isn't the only measure of inflation. RPI (retail price index) was the measure used until CPI was introduced and, unlike the CPI, it includes council tax and mortgage interest payments. RPI usually runs at a higher rate than the CPI. In practice, all measures of inflation can only be an average and the people who make up the average are likely to be experiencing their own inflation depending on what they spend their money on and by how much those purchases are going up.

Unfortunately, pensioners are often hit with personal inflation rates that are considerably higher than the reported rate of inflation. A larger than average proportion of pensioners' money is spent on energy bills and council tax, and these costs tend to increase above the average rate of inflation, as does the cost of domiciliary or residential care you might incur in later old age.

The Office for National Statistics has launched an interactive calculator on its website, www.statistics.gov.uk, that allows users to work out their own personal rate of inflation depending on how they actually spend their cash. It is worth carrying out this exercise to identify your own rate of inflation. It will act as your own personal benchmark to determine the return you need from your investments just to stand still!

11. Not being realistic

If an investment looks too good to be true, it probably is! If it's promising double-digit returns with no risk, look very closely at the small print. Maintain a degree of healthy cynicism. And don't invest in anything that you don't understand.

SUMMING UP

Taking control of your financial future is liberating. If you haven't done so already, start a savings regime. And if you are already saving, make sure that you're monitoring your current investment approach and making any necessary changes.

FURTHER READING

If you want to read more about investing, try the following selection:

William Bernstein: *The Four Pillars of Successful Investing*
John Bogle: *The Little Book of Common Sense Investing*
Charles Ellis: *Winning the Loser's Game*

Then, a little more complex for those who want to explore further:

Tim Hale: *Smarter Investing* (the only UK-centric book in this list)
Burton Malkiel: *A Random Walk down Wall Street*

USEFUL WEBSITES

Office of National Statistics (calculate your own, individual rate of inflation)	www.statistics.gov.uk
Money Facts	www.moneyfacts.co.uk
Money Made Clear	www.moneymadeclear.fsa.gov.uk

8

Equity release

'Paying for care is going to be a challenge and this is where this house comes in, it pays for that or its heirs and successors do.'

Sean Jeffries

USING YOUR HOME TO GENERATE AN INCOME OR CAPITAL

The home

Your home is probably the largest single asset that you own. By the time you retire the chances are that you will have paid off your mortgage and own your home outright. But how do you tap into the value of that asset to help fund retirement?

Well, you may be lucky, you may not need to use the value locked in your home to help fund your retirement plans. But, according to official government statistics, nearly six out of ten people defined as in poverty are homeowners. Recent (August 2008) statistics put the average house price in the UK at £185,000, and being able to utilize some of that value could make the difference between a comfortable retirement and a miserable one.

But a word of warning: don't rely on your home to provide you with your only source of retirement income. It may be necessary to try to unlock some of the equity tied up in your home to subsidize your retirement income but it should not be viewed as the only provision you are making. As we all know, the property market is not guaranteed only ever to move in an upward direction. And if you are a baby boomer when you are looking to realize some of the value in your home – so are all the other baby boomers. And markets can get depressed when there is a glut of supply…

Government help

Before you consider releasing the equity in your home, make sure that you are claiming all the benefits and/or grants you are entitled to from the State. Chances are you have paid your taxes and National Insurance and now might be pay-back time. Visit the Department for Works and Pensions at www.dwp.gov.uk and you can access information about benefits. For most benefits or entitlements you will have to contact your local office first; most benefits are dealt with at your local Jobcentre Plus office. For further information on where your local office is and how to contact it, see details under 'useful contacts' in Yellow Pages or under local office search at www.dwp.gov.uk.

Downsizing

When I talk to clients about the best way to release equity in their homes, the first thing I ask is: are they prepared to downsize? This is for two reasons. The first is not a financial one but to do with whether the house they currently live in is compatible with their long-term needs. It may be fine for them now when they are comparatively healthy, but what about later on? Is it close to shops and/or a bus route? Is the garden manageable? Is the house itself configured appropriately for someone with limited mobility? Is it draughty and expensive to heat? Depending on the answers to these questions, downsizing and looking for a more appropriate property might make sense. All too often people leave these decisions until the very last minute and then they don't have time to give due consideration to finding a new property; far better to do it too soon rather than too late.

I did have one client who, rather contrarily, said that everyone above a certain age should not live in a bungalow. He argued that living in a house with stairs kept you mobile for longer!

The second reason for giving priority to downsizing is a monetary one. It is often simpler and less costly to sell one home, buy a cheaper one and use the monetary difference to help fund retirement than it is to enter into an equity release arrangement. If the money isn't needed and inheritance tax is an issue then it can be gifted away. In addition, downsizing means that it is possible to retain ownership of 100 per cent of the home.

Having said all this, I am very aware of the emotional attachment people have to their homes; they are often places where they have lived for many years and built up memories that they would find hard to leave. Sometimes just the thought of having to clear the loft or the garage is enough to put people off moving house! So what other options are available?

Equity release

Equity release schemes got rather a bad reputation in the late 1980s when plans were sold that were not fit for purpose. These plans are no longer sold but it has left a bitter legacy and people have a mistrust of equity release schemes.

So what exactly is an equity release scheme? Equity release is the unlocking of some or all of the value tied up in a property, without the owner having to move house or being able to demonstrate that the money generated can be repaid out of income or savings. Borrowing money against the value of your home when you are older, often without the intention of ever repaying it until you die, might seem to fly in the face of conventional wisdom. However, it is becoming a more and more acceptable way of raising money to help fund the cost of retirement. And it is likely to become even more popular because baby boomers' attitude to debt is different from that of their parents, who would rather go without than be in debt. Baby boomers are not used to holding back – if they want something they will borrow, secured or unsecured, to get it.

Releasing equity in a house is often considered at a time when the homeowner is older and, perhaps, less able to cope with complex financial issues. And while there is no doubt that equity release has a valuable role to play in providing additional retirement income or capital, as always the watchword is: be careful. Make sure that the provider of any scheme used is a member of SHIP (Safe Home Income Plans). Members of SHIP have to conform to specific standards, including the permanent right to reside in the home, the right to move without financial penalty and a no-negative-equity guarantee. If you want to know more about SHIP, its website at www.ship-ltd.org is worth a visit.

It might be helpful if I explain what a no-negative-equity guarantee is. If you borrow a sum of money under a lifetime mortgage (see below), the sum originally borrowed, plus the interest payments, rolls up. This is referred to as compound interest because you are paying interest on rolled-up interest in addition to the sum borrowed. When the property is eventually sold, the sum realized should equal or exceed the sum originally borrowed plus compounded interest; if it doesn't and there is a shortfall then that is referred to as negative equity. However, if there is a no-negative-equity guarantee it means that the loan company cannot approach you or your estate for the shortfall; it has to bear the financial loss.

There are two types of equity release: home reversion and lifetime mortgages. The details provided below are very general. It is difficult to be specific as to whether equity release would be right for you and, if it were, which particular form would suit you, because it does depend so much on individual circumstances; for example: your age, marital status and your health. It also depends on what you want the money for: extra regular income, a one-off lump sum for a holiday, home improvements, to give to needy children, to help with inheritance tax planning or to fund the cost of long-term care. If you are interested in finding out more, talk to a financial planner who is experienced in, and qualified to advise on, equity release.

Home reversion schemes

- A home reversion scheme involves selling all or part of your home to a reversion company in exchange for a lump sum, an income (annuity) or both. You retain the right to live in the property for the rest of your life. If you have sold only a proportion of the property, you, or your estate, will benefit from the increase in value of the proportion you have retained ownership of.
- Usually the minimum sale is 30 per cent to 50 per cent of the property, although some reversion companies do have lower minimums. The maximum sale can be 100 per cent of the property, but again this will depend on the reversion company used; some have maximums slightly lower than 100 per cent, possibly on the basis that an individual retaining even a small interest in a property is likely to take better care of it!
- The home owner(s) are likely to receive between 25 per cent and 70 per cent of the market value of the proportion of the house they are selling; this is referred to as the price/market value ratio and can vary depending on the ages of the homeowner(s) and on their health, although a payment of more that 70 per cent of the value would be unusual.
- For example, a couple in their mid-60s with a house worth £200,000 sell 50 per cent of it to a reversion company. The price/market value ratio is 35 per cent so they would receive £35,000 for

the £100,000 of current value they are selling. If the value of the house had grown to £300,000 when it was sold the homeowners or their estate would receive £150,000 of the proceeds and the reversion company £150,000.

- It may seem a bit tough that the home reversion company pay only a percentage of the value. However, they may have to wait many years to see a return on their investment and they are taking a gamble that property prices will rise, by no means a certainty. In addition, they are allowing you to live, rent free, in a property of which they own a part or the whole. Obviously, the older you are the more money you are likely to get, because the reversion company have a shorter time to wait for a return on their investment.

- Generally you can borrow more under home reversion than you can under a lifetime mortgage, but that shouldn't blind you to the main drawback of these schemes: that you lose ownership of your home, or the proportion that you sell, to the home reversion company. You do need to feel comfortable with this aspect of home reversion. And, as an aside, any borrowing should be assessed on a needs basis rather than 'let's borrow the maximum'.

Lifetime mortgage

There are three different types of lifetime mortgage:

- roll-up lifetime mortgages;
- drawdown lifetime mortgages;
- home income plans.

Roll-up lifetime mortgage

Using a lifetime mortgage, the owner borrows against the value of the property, releasing a loan that can be used to provide an income (an annuity), a lump sum or both. Interest is rolled up and added to the outstanding loan. The loan does not have to be repaid until the owner dies or, in some cases, moves house, and the house is sold.

Drawdown lifetime mortgage

You agree with the mortgage company the maximum amount of borrowing against the property. However, initially only a proportion of the agreed loan is taken; the remainder is available to be drawn down at a later date as needs dictate. The advantage of this approach is that interest compounds only on that proportion of the loan that is taken, and on future sums only from the date that they are needed. Incidentally, it is possible to have a form of drawdown home reversion scheme.

Home income plans

A lifetime mortgage is used to release an agreed sum of money. Part of the sum released is used to buy an annuity that pays the interest on the loan. The argument is that you know where you stand because the loan isn't compounding into an unknown sum. However, I suggest that you approach such schemes with caution as you may find that the actual sum they provide for you to spend, over and above the sum needed to pay the interest on the loan, might be very small unless you are towards the older end of the age spectrum.

General comments on lifetime mortgages

- The interest rate on a lifetime mortgage can be fixed or capped. A recent survey carried out by SHIP indicated that the interest rates on lifetime mortgages are no more expensive than those on traditional residential mortgages. But it is worth shopping around, bearing in mind that interest rates are only one part of the picture.
- As with a home reversion scheme, the younger you are the less you can borrow. This is because the lender has to allow for the sum borrowed, plus the rolled-up interest, to be covered by the final sale of the house. The further away you are from dying the longer the compounding period for the interest and the greater the element of uncertainty over future house price inflation.
- As a general rule, someone in their early 60s can borrow up to about 20 per cent of the value of their property, subject to certain minimums. Someone in their mid-80s might be able to borrow up to 45 per cent of the value of their property.
- Don't underestimate the power of compounding interest! For example, if you had a fixed interest rate of 6.25 per cent on a compounding loan, the outstanding sum doubles in 12 years and trebles in 19 years. Any plan you consider should have a no-negative-equity guarantee so that you, or your estate, will not suffer financially if, when the house is sold, the sale value does not meet the outstanding loan plus rolled-up interest.
- The main advantage of a lifetime mortgage is that you don't lose ownership of your home. However, you have to be aware that the outstanding loan, plus compounded interest, may mean that

when your home is eventually sold the lender is owed all the proceeds and there is nothing left in the pot for you or your beneficiaries.

Issues to be aware of on both home reversion schemes and lifetime mortgages

- Check what the minimum/maximum ages are, as these do vary from lender to lender. Minimums can be 55 and maximums can be up to 85.
- What property criteria does the lender have? For example, most lenders will require the property to have little or no mortgage attaching and to be in a reasonable state of repair.
- It is likely that an independent valuation of the property will be needed. Check who will carry this out, what it will cost and who will pay for it.
- Do you have to keep the lender aware of changes in circumstances, for example death of a spouse and remarriage? What sort of information will they require?
- You will need legal advice. Check how this will be arranged, what it will cost and who will pay for it.
- Maintenance and repair of the property are important; often loans are contingent on repairs being undertaken, so check what these are. Home reversion scheme lenders can be very strict about maintenance and might even reserve the right to inspect the property to make sure that it is kept in a good state of repair.
- Check if you need to obtain consent from the lender to carry out structural alterations to the property in future eg add conservatory, patio, windows etc.
- Find out who is responsible for insuring the property.
- Are there any rules about leaving the property unattended for long periods of time, for example if you want to go on an extended holiday or it becomes necessary to have a long stay in hospital?
- How does the scheme cater for you moving house? Or moving into sheltered accommodation or residential care?
- What is the tax treatment of the sum you will receive? Equity released from a principal residence as a lump sum is not subject to capital gains tax, although check this out if part of the property has been used for business purposes or let out. Depending on where you invest the lump sum, and on your taxable status, the income it provides might be taxable. Where equity is released in the form of income (ie annuity), part of the income will be treated

as a return of capital and non-taxable but part will be classed as interest and, depending on your tax status, may be taxable.

- If you are eligible to receive means-tested welfare benefits, will these be adversely affected if you receive benefits from an equity release scheme?
- Are you in ill health? If so, make the potential lender aware of this, because some lenders specialize in lending more to people who have a reduced life expectancy owing to a medical condition. This can be especially beneficial if you are releasing equity from a house to help meet the cost of care home fees for the owner.
- Lifetime mortgages are a regulated area of business and, from April 2007, home reversion schemes have also been regulated. This is important because regulated business offers greater protection to the consumer.
- Finally – costs! There are costs associated with equity release: valuation fees, solicitor's fees, insurance, arrangement fees etc. Make sure that you are fully aware of the fees you will incur; costs do vary so shop around. Check if any of them can be added to the loan.

There are myriad equity release schemes on the market, some better than others. Take time to familiarize yourself with the basics of how equity release schemes work and do use a professional financial planner who is well versed in equity release and can steer you through the hype and help you choose the option that's right for you.

Ordinary mortgage

You could, of course, apply for an ordinary mortgage. Some lenders have quite high maximum ages for lending under a standard mortgage. You could take out an interest-only mortgage where the sum borrowed remains constant throughout the term and all you pay each month is the interest on it. When the mortgage comes to an end the sum owing to the lender is exactly the same sum as the one you borrowed.

Or you could take out a capital and repayment mortgage where, in addition to paying interest on the sum borrowed, you are also paying off some of the outstanding loan each month.

However, you would have to service the loan, so you would have to be confident that you could demonstrate to the lender that you had enough income to pay the interest, or the interest and an element of the outstanding loan, each month. If you had an interest-only mortgage you would also have to show that you had the means to repay the capital borrowed at the end of the term, but as the sum would be secured against your property the latter issue should not be a problem.

Why would you want a standard mortgage rather than a home reversion scheme or a lifetime mortgage? Well, you might not like the thought of selling part of your home to someone else under a home reversion scheme. Or you may not like the unquantifiable compounding of the interest on a lifetime mortgage. Also, there are fewer restrictions on a standard mortgage, for example if you want to pay off the borrowing sooner rather than later, move house, do alterations etc.

The major reason people opt for equity release is because they need extra money, so a standard mortgage would not suit them because they could not afford the regular payments on the loan. However, if you can afford the regular payments, and you think you might be eligible to take out a standard mortgage, there may be reasons for doing so.

For example, taking out a standard, interest-only mortgage on a property and then gifting away the sum borrowed can be quite an effective inheritance-tax-planning technique. As long as you live for seven years after making the gift it will be outside your estate for inheritance tax purposes. But to be effective, do remember that the gift has to be genuine; you cannot retain any ownership in the money or an asset that it buys. When you die the outstanding mortgage is a debt on your estate so will reduce your taxable estate accordingly. In addition, of course, the monthly payments to the lender will have reduced your estate further. Big word of warning – only pursue this course of action if you genuinely don't need the money the mortgage generates and can afford the monthly payments to the lender.

SUMMING UP

The above is only an overview of the issues you should consider if you are thinking about the possibility of releasing equity in your home. If you are serious about using your home to generate extra money, talk to an expert who can advise you specifically on the best course of action for you.

USEFUL WEBSITE

Safe Home Income Plans   www.ship-ltd.org

9

Pension planning

'When I left my job, and I'd been there more than 20 years, my brother-in-law asked only one question: "What about your pension?" And I said to him: "If I stay where I am I'm not even going to live to collect it, so I'm going." I thought, how boring of you; all you could think about was my pension!'

Joan Jarvis

INTRODUCTION

I wish I had £10 for every time I've heard the words 'pension' and 'boring' mentioned in the same sentence, because I would be a very wealthy woman! But let's face it, not having enough money to do what you want to do is pretty boring too. And although I agree with Joan that pensions are not the be all and end all of life, they do have an important role to play when you are making financial provision for your retirement, so please read on.

In this chapter I tackle three pension issues: how to find out what your current pensions are worth, how to make them worth more and how to take benefits from your pension funds. In an attempt to make this section of the book reasonably easy to understand I have had to simplify what is a very complex area and I do urge you to seek advice from a financial planner when tackling your pension planning.

But, before I start, I want to clear up one issue; I often hear the statement: 'Pensions haven't done very well, have they.' Let's get this straight: pensions are not a separate asset class, unlike equities or cash or fixed interest or property, which are separate asset classes. A pension is simply a tax-efficient investment vehicle for holding those separate asset classes. Some pensions have performed extremely well, some have performed very badly and the rest are somewhere in between. A pension will only perform as well as the investments that are held in it, so if the investments in your pension fund perform badly and the pension provider's charges are too high then, yes, you might be justified in telling me that *your* pension hasn't done well. But please don't absolve yourself of responsibility in all this. It is your responsibility to know where your pension is invested, how it is performing and how much you are paying the pension provider for the privilege of using their pension plan. OK – end of gripe.

WHAT ARE MY PENSIONS WORTH?

The State pension

A bit of history

Let's start with the State pension. The first State pension was introduced in 1908 for the over-70s. It was known as the 'Lloyd George Pension' and paid the princely sum of 5 shillings per week, 25p in today's money.

The current basic State pension scheme was introduced in 1948 and while it has undergone several changes since then, most of these have been tinkering around the edges. Give or take a bell or whistle, the structure of the basic State pension is roughly the same as it was in 1948, but since then demographics, lifestyles and expectations have changed.

So what's changed?

Employment patterns are different. People no longer spend their working lives with just one employer; they are likely to have a mix of several employers or employments, time off for travelling or to study, time out to care for children or elderly relatives.

Relationships have changed. People are far more likely to get divorced and remarry and have financial responsibility for more than one family. Also, we now have the legal entity of same-sex partners.

And people are living longer. In 1950 a man aged 65, the current State pension age, lived on average to age 76; now he can expect to live to 85 and it is projected that by 2050 it will be 89. Women can expect to live even longer.

The State pension scheme is a pay-as-you-go scheme. In other words, today's pensions are being paid for out of the money that to-day's workers contribute to the Chancellor's coffers. But the number of workers as a ratio to retired people is falling so there will be less going into the coffers to meet an increasing demand for payment. In 1950 there were five taxpaying workers for every pensioner, today there are three taxpaying workers for every pensioner and by 2050 it is projected that there will be one taxpaying worker for every pensioner.

The current State pension scheme is rooted in the society of the 1940s and society has moved on since then. Women in particular are disadvantaged by the current system, which does not work in favour of lower-paid, part-time workers who are likely to take time out of the workplace to care for children and elderly relatives. Indeed, of those recently reaching retirement age, 85 per cent of men are entitled to full State pension but only 30 per cent of women are.

What is the government doing about it?

The government has taken action. Under the banner of 'Security in retirement: towards a new pensions system', several reforms to the State pension are taking place to make it fairer for all. The reforms will not start to take effect until 6 April 2010. They include:

- Increasing the basic State pension by the rate of the increase in earnings. This should result in pensions increasing each year at a higher rate than they do presently, because current increases are in line with RPI (the retail price index) which generally runs at a lower rate than the increase in average earnings. It is planned that this change will take place some time between 2012 and 2014.
- Introducing a new system of credits that will increase the number of people who would become entitled to a State pension. This will be fairer, particularly for carers and part-time workers, and far more people than at present should be entitled to a full State pension.
- Increasing the State pension age from 65 to 68 between 2024 and 2046. Currently the State pension age for men is 65 and for women it is 60, but women's retirement age is being brought in line with that of men, phased in over the period 2010 to 2020.

Additional State pension

In addition to the *basic* State pension you may be entitled to additional State pension. This might include entitlement to benefits in the form of GRB (Graduated Retirement Benefits) if you paid enough contributions from April 1961 to April 1975. In 1978, SERPs (State Earnings Related Pension Scheme) was introduced and took the place of GRB. SERPs itself was replaced by S2P (State Second Pension) in 2002. Self-employed people cannot accrue additional State pension benefits.

You may have 'contracted out' of SERPs and the State Second Pension. If you have, this means that for the period you were contracted out you would not accrue additional State pension; instead, you would accrue benefits in the contracted-out scheme. If you did contract out at any stage, hopefully you have details of the period in question and the policy or scheme used to contract out. You can find out if you are contracted out at the moment by calling the HM Revenue & Customs contracted-out pension helpline on 0845 9150 150. Lines are open from 8am to 5pm, Monday to Friday, and you will need to quote your National Insurance number.

What does it all mean for me and how much State pension am I likely to get?

Confused? I am not surprised! And the basic and additional State pension schemes are only a part of it.

To find out how much State pension, both basic and additional, you are likely to receive at retirement, I recommend that you get a State pension forecast, sometimes referred to as a BR19. To do this you should contact the Retirement Pension Forecasting Team. Their telephone number is 0845 3000 168 or textphone 0845 3000 169. Lines are open from 8am to 8pm, Monday to Friday, and from 9am to 1pm on Saturdays. You can also get an online forecast or download a pension forecast application form at www.thepensionservice.gov.uk. In addition, you can ask the forecast team to prepare a projection for you based on 'what if' situations. For example, 'What if I decided to stop work at age 55 rather than age 65 – how would that affect the amount of State pension I would be entitled to receive?'

However, even if you qualify to receive it, the maximum basic State pension you can get is £90.70 per week (2008/09). You may, of course, be eligible to receive additional State pension on top of that.

Can I get more State pension?

You might be able to improve the amount of basic State pension you are due to receive by paying additional voluntary National Insurance contributions to buy extra years of 'credits'. The answers on your

BR19 form should tell you if you are eligible to buy extra years. But a word of warning here: as already mentioned, the government is changing the way in which the credit system for accruing State pension benefits works, so make sure that you are not paying for something that the government will be giving you for free somewhere down the line.

Should I put off claiming my State pension?

Good question! If you continue to work and earn an income after State retirement age you might not want to swell your taxable income with money that you don't need, so you might want to consider delaying taking the benefits from your State pension. If you do this you can gain extra pension or a taxable lump sum.

To gain extra pension you have to put off claiming your State pension for at least five weeks. For every five weeks you put off claiming you receive extra State pension of 1 per cent of your normal pension rate. This is the equivalent of about 10.4 per cent extra pension for every year you put off claiming. For example, say your State pension is £70 per week and you put off claiming it for two years, you will receive an additional weekly pension of £14.56.

To gain a taxable lump sum you have to put off claiming your pension for at least 12 months. The lump sum is calculated based on the amount of normal weekly State pension you would have received plus interest. The interest rate is always 2 per cent above the Bank of England base rate. For example, if the base rate is 4.5 per cent you would receive an interest rate of 6.5 per cent. In the above example, delaying receiving a pension of £70 per week for two years would give you a taxable lump sum of £7,760 based on an interest rate of 6.5 per cent.

Even if you have already started taking your State pension you could decide to stop it and build up extra State pension or a lump sum. There is no maximum deferment period.

Of course, this approach is not for everyone; many people need to take the money from their State pension as soon as they are entitled to receive it. But if you don't then it might be worth considering putting off claiming.

For more information there's a leaflet called 'How to get extra weekly State pension or a lump sum payment: your introduction to State pension deferral', leaflet number SPD2. You can get this free leaflet and many other helpful leaflets about State pension benefits from the Pension Service on 0845 7313 233 or its website at www.thepensionservice.gov.uk.

What about private pension provision?

Private pension provision includes pensions arranged by your employer, known as occupational pension schemes, as well as personal pensions. During a working lifetime it is possible to accumulate a conglomeration of private pension plans and these all need monitoring and assessing on a regular basis because they are likely to form the backbone of your income in retirement.

I am often shocked when I meet prospective clients by how little they know about their existing private pension provision and yet the total value of their pension funds can run into hundreds of thousands of pounds. Indeed, sometimes their pension fund is their second biggest asset after their house. And while they can usually tell me exactly what their house is worth, and how much its value has gone up, or down, since they bought it, very few can tell me where their pension funds are invested, the annualized rate of investment growth and what income the pension fund is on line to deliver to them when they retire.

So, to work!

Occupational pension schemes

Occupational pension schemes fall into two categories: final salary (defined benefit) or money purchase (defined contribution). There are one or two schemes that straddle both, but for the sake of this book I'm ignoring them.

Occupational pension schemes – final salary scheme

If you are fortunate enough to belong to a final salary occupational pension scheme, you are lucky indeed. A final salary pension scheme pays you a pension based on your final salary from the company and the number of years you have worked for the company. The pension you receive will usually increase in payment each year in line with some pre-ordained index and will usually make provision for a surviving spouse or partner's pension. You may be required to contribute to the scheme (contributory scheme) or you may not have to make any contributions (non-contributory scheme). Your employer takes all the investment risk of supplying you with the agreed pension.

What's happening to final salary pension schemes?

Unsurprisingly, final salary pension schemes are undergoing changes. Like the State pension scheme, these schemes were devised when the social demographics were very different from the ones we have today. Now that people are living to older ages in retirement, companies are worried about having to pay increasing pensions for far longer than originally envisaged. Wobbles in the stock market don't help either. Some of these pension funds are huge but they are vulnerable to market fluctuations in just the same way as every other investor. And the regulators are tough on these schemes, rightly so in many people's opinion, but it all contributes to the decision that many final salary schemes make, either to close or to change.

Yet many of the post-retirees I interviewed attributed their successful financial provision for retirement to their final salary pension. Here are just a few comments:

> Because my job gave me the pension it gave we've not spent any time worrying about financial planning for retirement.
>
> *Richard Jeffries*
>
> We've got a pension that covers all our expenditure so we don't have to worry.
>
> *Ernest Dennis*
>
> I never really did any financial preparation for retirement because I was of the view that I was in an excellent final salary pension scheme and that wasn't an incorrect view. Even now what we have in terms of pension hasn't fallen behind. We don't spend it all and we're fairly comfortable.
>
> *Sam Jarvis*
>
> We've just been very lucky, to be honest. The final salary pension – that was always there.
>
> *James Dent*
>
> I feel absolutely comfortable with the financial provision I've made, I feel very lucky because I have a good final salary pension.
>
> *Colin Matthews*

These people are indeed the lucky ones, and a dying breed. In future the true final salary pension scheme will be a rarity. This is one reason why I am writing this book; if people can no longer rely on a final salary pension, if they have to make their own provision for retirement, the sooner they start and the more they know about it, the better.

How do I know how much I'll get from my final salary pension scheme?

If you are a current member of a final salary pension scheme, your employer should send you a statement each year that shows you how much pension you can expect to receive from the scheme when you retire. If you haven't received one, ask your employer to send you one. The statement will make certain assumptions, for example that you stay with the company until the NRD (normal retirement date) of the scheme, usually 60 or 65. You are probably best placed to decide whether the assumptions used reflect reality. You also need to assess whether the scheme will remain unchanged between the date of the statement and your retirement; do not assume that it will.

What happens if I leave?

If you leave your employer before the normal retirement date of the scheme, either to take early retirement or move to another job, you become a deferred member of the final salary pension scheme. Provided that you are over 50 (you have to be over 55 from April 2010), you may be able to start taking your pension from the scheme when you leave, but check this out with your employer. Also, remember that if you do take your pension early you are likely to suffer an early retirement penalty that may result in you receiving a smaller pension.

If you don't take benefits you will remain a deferred member of the final salary pension scheme until the normal retirement date of the scheme. During deferment the benefits from the scheme should be increased each year. You should still receive an annual statement telling you what your pension is currently worth and what it might be worth at your normal retirement date. If you don't receive a deferred member benefit statement, ask for one.

Could I transfer my pension money out to another scheme?

Well, you could, but caution is urged here. You need to quantify exactly what you are giving up by transferring out of a final salary pension scheme and exactly what you are gaining in the new scheme. This is definitely one area where you should be seeking expert advice from a financial planner.

Occupational pension schemes – money purchase schemes

Money purchase schemes are not the unquantifiable commitment for an employer that final salary schemes are. This is because the amount of pension you receive at retirement depends on the total amount of money you and your employer have paid into the scheme over the years, how the underlying investments in the pension fund have grown and the annuity rates prevailing at the time you take your pension. It is the pot of money that the investments produce that is used to provide you with a pension.

How do I know how much I'll get from my money purchase scheme?

You should receive an annual statement. The projected pension in the statement will make assumptions, not only about how long you are likely to remain in the scheme and the contributions that will be paid but also the growth rate of the investments your pension fund is invested in and prevailing annuity rates.

What happens if I leave?

If you leave your employer before the normal retirement date of the scheme, either to take early retirement or move to another job, you become a deferred member of the money purchase pension scheme. Provided that you are over 50 (you have to be over 55 after 2010), you may be able to take your pension from the scheme when you leave, but check this out with your employer. Also, remember that if you do take your pension early you might suffer an early retirement penalty that may result in you receiving a smaller pension.

If you don't take benefits you will remain a deferred member of the money purchase pension scheme. Your deferred pension benefits from the scheme will increase (or decrease!) in line with the underlying investments. You should receive an annual statement telling you what your pension is currently worth and what it might be worth at your normal retirement date, using certain assumptions about the growth in value of the underlying investments and prevailing annuity rates.

Could I transfer my pension money out to another scheme?

Again the answer is yes, but I would still urge caution. Your employer may subsidize the cost of running the scheme, meaning that you are accessing investment funds more cheaply and paying lower annual management charges than you might with another scheme. There may also be other benefits that you would lose if you transferred out of the scheme.

Personal pensions

What types of personal pension are there?

You might have several personal pensions with several different providers. Personal pensions come in different guises:

- You might have one or more of the old-style personal pensions that were called RAPs (retirement annuity plans), sometimes known as Section 226 policies.
- SIPPs (self-invested personal pensions) are personal pensions.
- Stakeholder pensions are personal pensions with low charging and flexible structures but limited investment options.
- Your employer may sponsor, and possibly contribute to, a group personal pension of which you are member.
- If you decided to contract out of SERPs and/or the State Second Pension, as an individual rather than through a company scheme, the money you receive will have been invested in a personal pension, sometimes known as an appropriate personal pension.

The thing is that you need to be aware of every personal pension plan that you, your employer or the State has contributed to in the past and/or that you or they are contributing to now.

How do I know how much I'll get from my personal pensions?

The personal pension provider should send you an annual statement. This should tell you what your pension fund (ie the money invested in your personal pension plan) is currently worth, what it was worth 12 months ago and how much you have invested in the plan over the last 12 months. Hopefully the statement will also show you the percentage growth on your pension fund over the period.

If you took the personal pension plan out via a financial adviser or financial planner, they should receive annual statements on your behalf and provide you with analytical information about your pensions. If this isn't happening, get in touch with your adviser or planner and ask them for an update.

If your personal pension plan is a group personal pension plan sponsored by your employer, then your employer should provide you with an annual statement.

The annual statement you receive will also show a projection of the pension you can expect to receive at retirement. A few words of advice on these projections:

■ First of all, if you or your employer is still paying into the personal pension plan, the projected pension at retirement is likely to assume that the contributions continue. Indeed, in some cases you may have elected to pay regular contributions that increase each year and the projections will assume that the increases take place. So you need to make sure that you are comfortable with this assumption.

■ When you applied for your personal pension plan you would have been asked to nominate a retirement age; this would have been any age from 50 to 75. The projections will assume that you retire at the age originally nominated. How sensible is it to assume that you will retire at this age? Most personal pension plans are flexible enough to allow you to take your pension at a different age from that originally nominated, as long as it is between 50 (55 from April 2010) and 75, but check with the pension company; some of the older-style plans have slightly different rules and restrictions.

■ The projections have to assume certain growth rates in the underlying investments. Currently these growth rates are 5 per cent, 7 per cent and 9 per cent. The growth rate you choose to look at will depend on your own risk profile, how optimistic or pessimistic you are feeling about future investment returns and where the pension funds are invested. Obviously, if your pension fund is entirely in cash it is unlikely to achieve a 9 per cent return.

■ The pension that the projection shows you will receive at your nominated retirement age is likely to be shown in tomorrow's terms, which means it looks more impressive than it is. Between now and your retirement date inflation is likely to have eroded the value of the pension shown.

■ The projection is likely to assume that you buy a basic annuity at your nominated retirement age; this is not the only option that will be available to you at that time but for the sake of simplicity it is what the projection may use. An annuity is the financial device used to convert your pension fund into a regular pension income. Annuities come in all shapes and sizes – more on this later. The issue here is that there are different costs depending on the type of annuity bought. An annuity that pays you a regular income but stops when you die is cheaper than one that pays you a regular income but on your death continues to pay a regular income to a surviving spouse. Check what type of annuity the projection uses – is it appropriate for your circumstances?

■ If you have decided to contract out of the State Second Pension and consequently are accruing benefits in an appropriate personal pension plan, these benefits will be known as protected rights. There are slightly different rules governing how you can take the benefits from protected rights.

■ A final word of warning: some of the older-style pension plans, retirement annuity plans, had guaranteed annuity rates attaching to the policy. As already stated, an annuity rate is the rate used to convert a pension fund to pension income. Over the past two decades annuity rates have fallen quite dramatically, which means that you need a larger amount of pension fund than before to buy the same amount of pension income. Guaranteed annuity rates were part of many retirement annuity plans taken out in the early to mid-1980s when nobody believed that annuity rates would fall as low as they have. If you have a retirement annuity plan, check if it has guaranteed annuity rates. If it does, the rates are likely to give you a bigger pension than you could get elsewhere. But don't just check the amount of annuity the guaranteed rates give you, check how it is paid. Sometimes the guaranteed annuity rate option only gives you the very basic pension, payable from age 60 or later, with no option to choose such things as a spouse's pension, so it might not work for you.

If the assumptions the pension company have used when preparing their projections are not right for you, ask them to change them. The only assumptions they may not be able to change are the growth assumptions, because these are laid down by their regulators. You could, of course, set up your own spreadsheet and make your own assumptions and do your own projections.

Can I stop contributing to my personal pension?

Modern personal pension plans are extremely flexible but it is still worth checking just to make sure that there are no penalties or adverse implications of stopping paying into a pension plan; this is particularly important with older-style pension plans.

Can I consolidate my personal pensions?

Sometimes you can accrue so many different personal pension plans that it is difficult to keep track of them all. Consolidating all your personal pension plans into one or two plans may be a good idea, because it will ensure that you save time and the financial costs of administration. You should also be able to carry out a more meaningful asset allocation of the underlying investments in the pension plan and you might reap the benefits of an advantageous tiered charging structure. You may even decide to transfer your personal pension plans into a SIPP (self-invested personal pension plan); more on this later.

As always, the watchword is make sure that there are no penalties or other adverse implications by making the transfers.

Other issues on current pension provision

Can I take a pension from my occupational pension and continue to work?

It has always been possible to take a pension from your personal pension scheme, or from the State pension at State pension age, and to continue to work and this is still the case. It has also always been possible to take a pension from an occupational pension and continue to work – as long as you weren't working for the company where the occupational pension benefits came from.

The government has reviewed this decision. Demographics have played a part. Since 1997 the employment rate of those aged between 50 and State pension age has increased from 65 per cent to 70 per cent and currently more than a million people over State pension age are in work.

The government is keen to encourage this trend by making the pension regime flexible and to keep everyone in work for as long as possible, not just because people in work are less of a financial drain on the State but because there appears to be evidence to show that having an occupation enhances well-being and saves the NHS money.

The upshot of all this is that it is now possible to take a pension under an occupational pension scheme and to continue to work for the employer who provided it. This will certainly help those who want to subsidize their pension in the early years of retirement by working, possibly part time, at a job they know and enjoy.

Consolidated pension statements

The government has been keen to introduce a system of consolidated pension statements and forecasts. The idea is that you will have one statement that captures all your pensions, State, occupational and personal, and combines them to give you one projected pension income figure at retirement. Unfortunately, we are still a long way off achieving this, so you will have to put in some spade-work to arrive at a projected pension income figure from all your pension schemes.

What if I can't find details of some of my past pension plans?

This happens a lot. We have become an itinerant workforce, so it is very easy for someone to be a member of an occupational pension scheme for a few years early in their career, leave and subsequently lose track of the pension scheme. Or to take out a personal pension plan for a few years, only to let it lapse when circumstances change. Fortunately, there is a Pension Tracing Service that will help you find any old occupational or personal pension plans. You can contact them by telephone on 0845 6002 537 or textphone 0845 3000 169. Lines are open from 9am to 5pm, Monday to Friday. You can also fill in the pension tracing request form online at www.thepensionservice.gov.uk or write to:

The Pension Tracing Service
Tyneview Park
Whitley Road
Newcastle upon Tyne NE98 1BA

HOW DO I MAKE MY PENSION WORTH MORE?

Should I be trying to make my pension worth more?

First of all, let's address the question of: 'Should you be trying to make your pension worth more?' Making financial provision for your retirement isn't just about piling money into pension plans. An effective investment plan for retirement will encompass saving into several different investment vehicles of which pensions are just one. Each investment vehicle has pros and cons but having a basket of them means you are less likely to be at the mercy of the cons.

Advantages and disadvantages of pensions

The advantages of saving money into a pension plan are mostly around the tax relief available, although there are other advantages:

- Money you pay into a pension plan is given tax relief at the rate of income tax you pay. So, depending on your income level, if you are a 40 per cent taxpayer, every £100 paid into a pension should only cost you £60. If you are a basic-rate taxpayer, every £100 paid into a pension will only cost you £80 (from 6 April 2008).
- Once invested, the money in a pension fund grows in a tax-advantaged environment.
- When you take benefits from your pension fund you are usually able to take 25 per cent of the total fund tax free.
- Until you start to take benefits from your pension plan the fund itself is usually outside your estate for inheritance tax purposes and should therefore pass to your beneficiaries tax free.
- Saving into a pension fund is a good discipline for retirement provision.

The disadvantages of pensions are:

- You cannot access the money in a pension before age 50 (age 55 from April 2010).
- And even when you can access it you have the take the benefits in a certain way. While you are usually allowed to take up to 25 per cent of the total fund tax free, the remainder must be used to provide you with an income which will be taxed as earned income.

Pensions are seen as inflexible and complex and, to a degree, they are. But the tax reliefs available on pensions savings, coupled with the enforced discipline of leaving your money untouched, make them a good long-term investment plan for retirement.

So how do I make my pension worth more?

There are two ways to make your pension plans worth more. The first is to review your current pension plans; look at what they are worth and where they are invested and determine if they could be invested in a better way to give you greater growth and a bigger fund. This approach will only work if you have some control over where your pension fund is invested, either because it is in a money purchase

occupational pension scheme where you are allowed some investment choice, or it is in some form of personal pension plan.

The second way to make your pension plans worth more is to pay
more into them.

How do I review my current pensions?

Generally, the advice that follows in this section does not relate to final
salary occupational pension schemes because in these schemes the
employer (via pension trustees), not the scheme member, is responsible for monitoring the scheme and making sure that it will provide
the promised pension.

Where an occupational pension scheme is a money purchase
scheme it is likely that the scheme member will have some choice over
which investments their pension fund is invested in. However, there
may be a limited choice of investment options, so you need to be
aware of this. The important thing is that you know what your investment options are and have sufficient information about them to make
an informed choice.

Your aim is to try to find out what your total pension fund from all
your pension plans is worth, where it is invested, how it is performing
and what you are paying the pension company or companies for
looking after it all. Armed with this information you may be quite able
to carry out an assessment of your current pension fund. Your pension
'fund' is the pot of money that your pension plans are invested in and
comprises various investment assets eg cash, equities, fixed interest,
property etc.

The assessment should include finding out the split of your pension
fund; by this I mean how much is invested in cash, how much in equities, how much in fixed interest etc. How does this fit in with your
time horizon and appetite for risk? If you are retiring in two years'
time you might not be happy if the entire fund is in high-risk equities;
what would happen if they fell in value by 50 per cent between now
and your retirement date? On the other hand, if you are 20 years away
from retirement you might not want your entire pension fund to be
sitting in cash.

Ideally the assessment should also include an analysis of the
performance of the underlying investments in your pension fund.
And it should also include details of the charges you are paying the
pension company and how these compare with other pension companies' charges. However, I appreciate that this data may not be easy to
come by.

Once you have this information you can decide what you are going to do. You might be quite happy just to leave things as they are. But if you want to make changes, what are your options? Well, you can consider leaving your pension fund with the current pension company but carry out some fund switches. A fund switch is where you move some, or all, of your pension money from one investment fund to another. For example, you might want to switch out of the Far Eastern Precipice fund into cash or, indeed, vice versa! Check what costs you will incur for making switches and make sure that there are no adverse implications for your pension fund if you were to carry out switches.

Alternatively, you might want to consider moving your pension plan to another provider or, if you have more than one pension plan, consolidating them into one scheme. Again, care is needed. Make sure you know what the charges are for moving your pension plan. And also make sure that you don't lose any benefits or trigger any detrimental effects to your entire pension planning by carrying out the move.

The above may seem complex and I wouldn't want to put you off reviewing your current pension provision because you feel that you would have to get a degree in Advanced Maths before tackling it! Sometimes just finding out what your current pension provision is worth, where it is invested and promising yourself to keep better track of it in future is enough to give you peace of mind and make you feel more in charge of your own destiny.

How do I pay more into my pensions?

Fewer and fewer people are saving into pensions; the government call it 'retirement under-saving'. Anxious to find out what had caused this inertia on the part of the electorate, the government commissioned a survey that revealed that people just don't trust private pensions, they feel there's a lack of suitable savings vehicles and the pension system is too complex. Well, pensions are complex but with a bit of perseverance, or help, they are understandable. I think that there are many good pension companies out there offering excellent pension savings vehicles. And I think trust comes through understanding and knowledge, because that allows you to take control and make sensible choices.

Another reason people are reluctant to save into pensions is because they worry that they may lose additional means-tested retirement benefits if they have made private provision; why incur the cost of saving and making private provision if it is just replacing something they'd get for free via State benefits? Well, I can understand why that would make someone think twice about saving into a pension. And you do need to make sure that you are not losing out on means-tested benefits by saving. But situations change and the government are reviewing their stance on means-tested retirement benefits, so bear that in mind when deciding if saving into a pension plan is worth it.

Within the next few years the government plans to introduce personal accounts, a new low-cost pensions savings scheme. The plan is that they will be high-quality, low-cost savings vehicles. But the introduction of these plans is some way away, so what do you do now if you want to increase your pension benefits by saving more? That will depend on what pension planning you are currently undertaking.

Occupational pensions

What if I am in a final salary pension scheme or have the opportunity to join such a scheme?

Generally speaking, if you have the opportunity to join a final salary pension scheme, bite your employer's hand off. But accept that the rules governing the scheme may have to change in the future to accommodate the demands of an ageing membership. Don't be put off joining an occupational pension scheme because of the cases where companies have reneged on their pension promises. These are isolated incidents that just happen to have high-profile exposure in the press. The government is trying to address the issue by providing protection to members of occupational pension schemes that cannot meet their obligations. There is the Financial Assistance Scheme and the Pension Protection Fund which, arguably, have made final salary pension schemes safer than they have ever been.

What about money purchase occupational pension schemes?

Again, the rule of thumb is that if you have an opportunity to join such a scheme then you should join. Your employer will make contributions into the scheme on your behalf, the cost of the scheme is likely to be subsidized by the employer and there may be other benefits associated with the scheme.

Can I pay more into an occupational pension scheme?

It might be possible for you to pay additional contributions into an occupational pension scheme to increase your likely benefits and you might want to ask about this. In some cases your employer might be prevailed upon to match, up to a certain amount, the additional money that you pay in.

Alternatively, you might want to take out a personal pension and save into that alongside the occupational scheme.

Can I contribute to a personal pension if I am a member of an occupational pension scheme?

In addition to being a member of an occupational pension scheme, you can contribute to a personal pension at the same time and you might want to consider doing this. Be careful that after taking account of the annual benefits you are accruing in the occupational pension scheme, or any other pension scheme, you are not over-contributing into the personal pension plan. If you are, you may not receive tax relief on the contributions or may even incur a tax penalty. However, the contribution limits are generous, basically the lower of your earnings or £235,000 (2008/09), £245,000 (2009/10).

And bear in mind that you will have to shoulder the full cost of a personal pension plan because your employer will not subsidize the costs of the plan in the same way they would an occupational pension scheme.

Personal pensions

What about paying more into a personal pension?

Few people are paying the maximum they can into pensions, so if you have a personal pension you might want to find out about paying more into it and increasing your pension benefits that way. Before you do this I suggest that you make sure that you are happy with your current personal pension arrangements; you don't want to feel that you are throwing good money after bad. Deciding to pay more money into a personal pension plan is often a good opportunity to review your pension planning as a whole, so that you can make sensible decisions about exactly where the new contribution is going to be invested.

Employers can make contributions into a personal pension plan on your behalf. Indeed, you may already be a member of a personal pension plan that your employer is contributing into. But if not, and you have some sway within your organization, you might want to ask your employers if they would be willing to contribute to a personal pension plan on your behalf. A particularly effective way for an employer to contribute into your personal pension plan is via a salary or bonus sacrifice, where you waive the right to part or the whole of a future bonus or salary increase and have it paid into your personal pension plan. The immediate benefit is a saving in National Insurance but there is also the benefit of not missing what you've never had! There are specific rules governing salary and bonus sacrifice so make sure that you're following these if you decide that this is something you would like to do. Of course, you need to feel confident that your financial situation is such that you wouldn't miss the money you've sacrificed.

How much can I pay into a pension plan?

In any one year you can pay as much as you like into a personal pension plan. However, there are limits on the amount of tax relief given. Broadly speaking, you can get tax relief on contributions up to 100 per cent of the lower of your earnings or £235,000 (the annual allowance for 2008/09) or £245,000 (the annual allowance for 2009/10). The same allowances apply to contributions into occupational pension schemes. However, contributions into an occupational pension scheme are likely to be governed by funding limits particular to that scheme, although you could, of course, save into a personal pension plan alongside the occupational pension scheme to maximize tax relievable contributions. If you are accruing benefits in an occupational pension and funding a personal pension plan at the same time then the one limit applies to both.

There is also a lifetime allowance on the amount you can accumulate in all your pension funds when you come to take benefits without incurring an additional tax charge. For 2008/09 this is £1.65 million and for 2009/10 it is £1.75 million.

Both the annual allowance and the lifetime allowance are due to increase each year until 2010/11 when the situation will be reviewed.

Other issues on making my pension worth more

What if I don't have a pension plan?

Then you might want to consider taking one out. First of all, find out if your employer has a scheme that you can join. If not, think about taking out a personal pension.

How do I choose a good personal pension plan?

It is always worth shopping around to find a personal pension plan that suits you. Charges are important, so try to compare the various charging structures of the different pension companies. You can ask them to prepare quotes for you based on you paying either a regular monthly or annual sum into the plan or just a one-off lump sum. The quotation should include a figure called the reduction in yield figure. This figure shows you the percentage reduction to your gross return that is eaten up in charges, in other words what is being taken off your bottom line. Obviously the lower this figure is the better. Ideally you are looking for a reduction in yield figure of around 1 per cent or even less. If you want access to a wider and more sophisticated range of funds you might have to accept a greater cost and, therefore, a higher reduction in yield.

Flexibility is important too. What are the minimum contributions? Can you stop and start premiums without having to pay a penalty?

Check out the investment funds available in the personal pension plan. You might be happy to settle for just one or two in-house funds, in other words funds run by the pension company, or you might want access to a range of external funds run by other investment houses as well.

If you have access to the internet there are several websites that help you sift through the information available about the various pension companies and make comparisons, but do make sure that they haven't got an axe to grind and are pushing you in the direction of some sponsoring provider.

If the amounts you pay into a personal pension plan are likely to be small and you want lots of flexibility over when and how much you pay into your pension plan, a stakeholder pension plan, one type of personal pension plan, might be a good choice for you. The following characteristics apply to stakeholder pension plans:

- The charges are capped; there are limits to how much you have to pay the pension company in charges.
- There are low minimum contribution levels.
- They are more flexible than many other personal pension plans; you can choose when and how often you pay into the plan and there are no penalties if you miss a payment.
- Other people as well as you and your employer can pay into a stakeholder pension plan on your behalf. This means that partners or other family members can help you to save for your retirement.

■ However, the investment options within a stakeholder pension plan might be limited to just one or two funds, so you would need to be happy about this.

What if I don't have an income?

You don't have to be earning an income to have a pension. You can take out a personal pension and pay up to £3,600 into it each year and receive tax relief on the contribution even if you don't pay tax. In other words, if you were paying the maximum you would pay £2,880 into the pension plan and the government would pay in the other £720 to make it up to £3,600. The tax relief is valuable and if you can afford to take out such a plan you should consider it. However, bear in mind that there are restrictions that apply on when and how you can access your pension savings, so you might not want to do this at the expense of, say, building up a cash emergency fund.

Also, you need to bear in mind that making provision for a private pension might adversely affect your ability to receive means-tested benefits in retirement, although, as already pointed out in this chapter, the government is reviewing its stance on means-tested benefits.

You might be ignoring saving into a pension plan or, indeed, carrying out any savings because you have a rich spouse who will look after you in your old age. Well, that's good news but remember that situations change. And if you have made provision for your own income in retirement and the situation doesn't change, when you ride off into the sunset together you'll each have savings in your own right generating an income that will be using your tax allowances much more effectively than if just one of you had all the money.

I've heard a lot about SIPPs – should I have one?

SIPPs are self-invested personal pension plans and there is nothing mystical about them. A SIPP is simply a personal pension plan on which you, or you and your adviser, make all the investment decisions.

But SIPPs are not for everyone. They can be expensive and, while this expense might be justified if you want to take advantage of the full range of investments you are permitted to hold within a SIPP, the costs may not be justified if you are holding a few unit trusts or insured pension funds. So first of all, decide if you are going to take advantage of the wider investment remit provided within a SIPP, which as well as investments into unit trusts, shares and cash investments includes such things as commercial property. If not, you might want to stick with a standard personal pension.

If you are considering taking out a SIPP, do check with your chosen provider what investments they allow you to hold within their SIPP. Not all providers are what I term full SIPP providers; several offer only a halfway house where some investments, while legally permitted to be held within a SIPP, are not catered for by that particular provider. For example, you might be keen to hold a commercial property in your SIPP and it would be disappointing to say the least to find out, once you had taken out your SIPP, that your chosen provider did not allow commercial property as an investment asset in their particular SIPP.

Some of the online SIPP providers are very cost effective and easy to use. And if you want to hold a basket of shares within your SIPP, the online dealing facilities are on hand. But while they are very cost effective, many online SIPP providers have a limited investment range, so check this out before signing up to make sure that you can hold all the assets you want to hold.

SIPPs work better for larger sums of money. It stands to reason that if you want to take advantage of the full range of permitted investments you are going to need a reasonable amount of money in your pension fund. In my view SIPPs are not really appropriate for pension funds worth less than £100,000.

Also, the charging structure of SIPPs works better with larger sums because some of the fees tend to be flat charges, especially annual fees levied by the pension company. Do make sure that you know exactly what you are letting yourself in for with SIPP charges, because quite often there will be several: financial planner, investment adviser, dealing fees, pension company fees, property manager fees etc. But the good thing about SIPP charges is that you usually know exactly what you are paying, unlike several insured pension contracts where it is almost impossible to calculate what the total cost is.

From April 2007 the Financial Services Authority has been monitoring SIPPs and this should lead to improved consumer protection and more transparent business practices. You can check if a SIPP provider has received approval from the FSA by visiting www.moneymadeclear.fsa.gov.uk.

SIPPs are great if you want to be in control of your own pension fund, have a pension fund in excess of £100,000, want to take full advantage of allowable pension investments and are aware of, and happy to pay, the associated costs.

Summing up on how do I make my pensions worth more with a word of caution

As I said at the beginning, saving into pensions is only part of the discipline of saving for retirement. The pro of pensions is the tax relief and the discipline of saving. The inflexibility of pensions, ie not being able to get your hands on the money and having to take it in a prescribed way, is the con of pensions. So don't put all your savings into pensions; make sure that you build up a cash emergency fund and, if possible, that you have other monies in investments that you can get your hands on in times of need.

HOW DO I TAKE BENEFITS FROM MY PENSION PLANS?

Introduction

In an effort to make pensions more attractive the government is keen to increase the number of options people have when it comes to converting their pension funds into an income stream. However, as so often happens, increasing the number of options also increases the difficulties in choosing the one that's right for you.

As I have already pointed out, in an effort to preserve some comprehension in this part of the book I have had to simplify what is a very complex subject. Again, this is definitely one area where I do urge you to take advice from a financial planner. A financial planner will research the market on your behalf and ensure that you convert your pension funds into an income stream on the most appropriate and beneficial terms for you.

Taking benefits

When can I take benefits from my pension funds?

You can take pension benefits between the ages of 50 (55 from April 2010) and 75.

If you have an occupational pension scheme, the date for taking benefits will usually be determined by the scheme trustees and is referred to as the NRD (normal retirement date). NRD is usually somewhere between 60 and 65. You may be able to take benefits from the scheme before the normal retirement date but not before age 50 (55 from April 2010). However, if you do this then the chances are that you will suffer an early retirement penalty that will reduce your pension payments. You might be able to delay taking benefits beyond the normal retirement date but this will depend on the scheme rules.

If you have a personal pension you can choose when to take benefits, provided that this is between the ages of 50 (55 from April 2010) and 75. But remember that the earlier you take benefits the less time your pension fund will have to grow in value so the less pension income it will provide. Also, the younger you are the lower the annuity rates are. Annuity rates are the rates used to convert your pension fund into pension income; more about annuities and annuity rates later.

Do I have to take all my pension benefits at once?

If you have several pension plans you might be able to take benefits from each one at different times. Even if you have just one pension plan, if it is a personal pension, the chances are that it is divided into several sub-policies or segments and it is usually possible to take benefits from one or more segments while leaving the remaining ones invested.

The advantages of not taking all your pension benefits at once are:

- You don't have to take more pension income than you actually need. If you are continuing to work part time you might simply be looking for enough pension income to help subsidize your earnings rather than increase your income tax bill.
- Those plans, or segments of a plan, that remain invested will hopefully continue to grow in value. And annuity rates might improve because you will be older when you take the remaining benefits, ultimately resulting in a higher level of income from the pension fund left invested.
- Also, those plans, or segments of a plan, from which you have not taken any benefits are likely to be outside your estate for inheritance tax purposes. You might view this as an advantage, which indeed it can be. However, be aware that the Inland Revenue takes a dim view of you not taking benefits from your pension funds if you have reached retirement age and know that you are likely to die within the next year or two. This is especially so if it is obvious that you have delayed taking benefits simply with a view to passing on the money within your pension fund, tax free, to someone other than a dependant.

The disadvantages of not taking all your pension benefits at once are:

■ Those plans, or segments of a plan, that remain invested might fall in value, annuity rates might worsen and you'll have missed out on the income that the still invested pension could have produced.

I never said any of this was easy!

So, what are my options for taking benefits?

That depends on what type of scheme you are in:

■ If you are in a final salary occupational pension scheme, your pension will be calculated depending on your years of service and salary in the formula that pertains to the scheme. And when you retire your pension is then usually paid from the scheme.
■ If you are in a money purchase occupational scheme, your pension will be calculated depending on the value of the investments accumulated in your pension fund and what income that can buy using current annuity rates. When you retire, your pension may be paid either from the scheme or from an insurance company that offers competitive annuity rates.
■ If you have a personal pension plan, your pension will depend on the value of the investments accumulated in your pension fund and what income that can buy using current annuity rates. An insurance company that offers competitive annuity rates will pay your pension.
■ If you have a personal pension plan, rather than converting your pension fund to an income stream via an annuity you may be able to leave the pension fund invested and draw an income from it; more on this later. This ability is also available on certain types of money purchase occupational pension schemes.
■ If you have an older-style pension, a retirement annuity, you may have guaranteed annuity rates attaching which could give you a higher level of income but usually only payable from age 60; see 'How do I know how much I'll get from my personal pensions?' above. If you want to take advantage of the guaranteed annuity rates, the insurance company that your pension fund is invested with will pay your pension.

In all the above you will have the option to forego some of the pension income and take a tax-free cash lump sum instead, referred to as a pension commencement lump sum. In most cases this will be 25 per cent of the value of the fund but there are a few occasions where it may be a different percentage and this is something that you should check out.

Should I take the tax-free cash from my pension, now known as a pension commencement lump sum?

Well, this will depend on your individual circumstances, but generally my answer is yes, you should. Any pension income you receive is taxed as earned income. If you commute some of that income for a tax-free pension commencement lump sum, you have the opportunity to use that lump sum in a number of ways. You might want to earmark it for a capital expenditure item. Alternatively, you might want to invest it tax-efficiently, for example in a capital growth investment where gains are taken, offset against your annual capital gains tax exemption, and spent as tax-free 'income'. Or you might want to give it to a spouse whose income tax rate is lower than yours so that he or she can invest it for income and use more of his or her lower-rate income tax bands. Or, if you can afford to, you might want to gift it away to benefit others and reduce your estate for inheritance tax purposes. As you can see, the tax-free pension commencement lump sum bristles with opportunities denied to an income stream!

There are exceptions to the above and one of these is if you have a retirement annuity policy with guaranteed annuity rates where the rate for converting the pension fund to income is so attractive it is hard to consider giving some of it up.

What exactly is an annuity and what's so important about annuity rates?

A lifetime annuity is a regular income, guaranteed for life, bought with your pension fund and referred to as a pension. An annuity rate determines how much income you get in exchange for your pension fund; the lower the annuity rate the less pension income you can buy.

Annuity rates are currently pretty low. This is because the yields on government gilts that determine annuity rates are low and, in addition, the actuaries who fix annuity rates have to take into account that people are living longer so the pension income will have to pay out for more years. This situation is unlikely to improve in the short to medium term:

■ Your age and sex will affect what annuity rate you receive. Usually the older you are the higher the annuity rate and consequently the higher your pension income because it has to be paid for a shorter time.

■ Men usually secure higher annuity rates than women of the same age because they have a shorter life expectancy.

■ Your health will also affect the annuity rate. If you have suffered an illness that is likely to shorten your life expectancy, you may qualify to receive an impaired-life annuity. An impaired-life annuity will give you a higher rate of income because it is assumed that you will die sooner than a healthy person of your age.

■ Your lifestyle could also influence what annuity rate you receive. For example, if you are a smoker you may qualify for a higher annuity rate, or similarly if you live in a geographical area of the country where life expectancy is lower than the average.

■ Finally, how you decide to take your pension income will determine the annuity rate you receive: see below.

As you can see, there is more to annuity rates than meets the eye, so do be aware of these issues when you are researching converting your pension fund into pension income.

How do I know how much income I'll get from a lifetime annuity?

When you are coming up to the selected retirement age for your pension plan the pension company will write to you with a list of your options. One of those options will be to buy an annuity with that particular company. If the pension company hasn't written to you, perhaps because you haven't yet reached the selected retirement age, you can ask for details of your pension fund value and what pension income it might buy you now; assuming of course that you are 50 (55 from April 2010) or over.

Then – shop around! You do not have to buy your pension income from the company where your pension plan is invested. This ability to buy your pension income from the company with the best annuity rates is called the open market option, or OMO. It might be that the company where your pension plan is invested does have the best annuity rates, but you won't know that until you have compared rates. And there can be up to 30 per cent difference in the best and worst annuity rates.

There are many websites dedicated to providing information about annuity rates, but care is needed to make sure that you are comparing like with like.

A word of warning: if you have an old-style personal pension, known as a retirement annuity, and it has guaranteed annuity rates, you will lose these if you buy your annuity from a different company from the one your retirement annuity plan is invested with.

What form does the pension income take?

When you come to buy your pension you will have various options that allow you to tailor your future income to meet your own circumstances.

Married or single

If you are married and have a spouse or a civil partner, you might want to make provision for a pension for them in the event that you die first. You can choose to buy a pension that on your death continues to pay a pension to your surviving spouse either at the rate it was being paid to you, or at a reduced rate expressed as a percentage of your pension eg 50 per cent spouse's pension. This is referred to as a joint life annuity.

If part of your pension is comprised of protected rights accumulated as a result of your decision to contract out of the State Second Pension, and you are married or have a civil partner, then you have to buy a 50 per cent spouse's or partner's pension with that part of your pension.

Guaranteed period

As long as you live an annuity will pay you the promised income, but what happens if you die shortly after buying your pension? Well, you can choose to buy a guaranteed period for your pension of up to 10 years. This means that if you die before the guaranteed period ends the income payments will continue to be paid, at the rate they were being paid to you before you died, until the end of the period. And it may be possible to convert the remaining payments into a lump sum.

Increasing pension

A basic annuity pays a level pension; this means that the regular pension income you receive at the beginning remains the same until you die. You might be quite happy with this or you might want to consider buying an income that increases in payment each year. You can link the increase to a flat percentage, say 3 per cent, or you can link it to the increase in the retail price index each year. While you will receive a lower initial pension if you choose one that increases in payment, your income, and therefore your purchasing power, is less likely to be eroded by inflation.

But check the figures out, using various assumptions about inflation. This will help you determine the cross-over period when the increasing pension is paying more than the level one, in terms of both the regular amounts and total payments to date.

Regularity of payment

Decide when you want to receive your pension income. You could have it paid monthly, three- or six-monthly or annually. You can also choose to have the payment made at the beginning of the period – in advance, or at the end of the period – in arrears.

Annuity protection

It is possible to protect the sum remaining in your annuity if you were to die before age 75. This is sometimes called a value-protected or money-back annuity. They work as follows: if you die before age 75, the total of the pension payments you received during your lifetime is deducted from the value of the pension fund used to buy the annuity. The sum remaining is called an annuity protection lump sum death benefit (pause for breath) and is returned to your family less a 35 per cent tax charge.

An example might help. Let's say your pension fund is worth £100,000 and paid a pension income of £6,000 per annum and you died after 6 years. The total payments made would have been £36,000. This is deducted from the £100,000 leaving £64,000. From this sum is deducted the 35 per cent tax charge, leaving £41,600 to be paid out to your family.

Important to remember

The important thing to remember is that whatever options you choose for taking your pension income there is a cost. The cheapest annuity, and the one that provides the highest initial level of income, is the single life annuity ie one that dies with you, is paid once a year in arrears, has no guarantees or protection and does not increase each year in payment. Now, receiving your pension income in this way might suit you down to the ground but it might not.

Choosing options other than the basic ones will have the effect of reducing your initial pension. For example, choosing a pension where the payments increase each year in line with RPI can have the effect of reducing your initial pension by up to 35 per cent. I am not saying that you shouldn't choose any of the above options; they are likely to be of benefit to a great many of you. I just think you need to be aware of the cost and the implications for your retirement income planning.

Finally, the most important thing to remember is that a lifetime annuity gives you certainty. There is great peace of mind that comes from knowing that your pension income is guaranteed until you, and also your spouse if you so choose, die. I cannot overemphasize the value of this aspect of lifetime annuities and urge you to bear it in mind when you are making choices about how to convert your pension fund into income.

How much income can I expect from a conventional annuity?

This will depend on how you decide to take the income from your pension. As you can imagine, the permutations are endless and annuity rates fluctuate from day to day so it would misleading to include examples. However, current annuity rates are often shown in the financial pages of newspapers or in financial magazines. Also, there are several websites which will give you access to current annuity rates.

Are there only conventional lifetime annuities available?

In addition to conventional lifetime annuities, you could use your pension fund to buy an investment-linked lifetime annuity. Investment-linked annuities are similar to conventional annuities in that you receive a pension income in return for your pension fund. The difference is that the pension fund used to buy the income remains invested with the aim of growing in value, so that in future it might provide you with a higher level of income. Investment of your pension fund could be in an insurance company's with-profits fund or in unit-linked funds.

This approach might appeal to you, but do remember that an investment-linked lifetime annuity does not have the same security provided by a conventional lifetime annuity ie knowing that your income is guaranteed for life. If the underlying investments in an investment-linked annuity under-perform, you could see your pension income fall. In addition, there are ongoing costs and charges for dealing with an investment-linked annuity which have to be taken into account when calculating the return.

Again, this is an area where you should seek advice from a financial planner.

And remember that you can mix 'n' match. If you have more than one pension fund, or one pension fund that is split into segments, you can take different approaches to securing an income with the different pots.

What's this about drawing an income from my pension plan?

If the idea of buying a lifetime annuity doesn't appeal then you might want to consider an unsecured pension.

Unsecured pensions come in two forms: income withdrawal or short-term annuities.

What's income withdrawal?

With income withdrawal your pension fund remains invested in a tax-advantaged environment and you take a pre-agreed level of income direct from it. The income is taxed as earned income.

The amount of income you can take is between 0 and 120 per cent of the income you could get from a level, single-life lifetime annuity for a person of your age and sex. This means that you could take the pension commencement lump sum from your pension fund but no income, although this approach needs careful consideration.

HMRC (Her Majesty's Revenue & Customs) review the level of income you can take every five years. You can choose to have a review of the maximum level of pension you can take on any anniversary of it starting, instead of having to wait for five years, and you can change the amount of income you are withdrawing, provided you don't exceed the maximum 120 per cent. This will enable the pension to more closely follow the investment returns achieved by the schemes. The five-yearly review still happens if there have been no reviews in the meantime. But it is important to remember that you should not leave it for five years before reviewing your income withdrawal levels and the pension fund you are withdrawing it from. You can review and change the funds your pension fund is invested in and these regular reviews are important, because over time your situation will change and investment markets will change.

You can stop income withdrawal at any time and use your remaining pension fund to buy a lifetime or short-term annuity; see below for more on short-term annuities. By age 75 you must secure an income from your pension funds, which generally means buying a lifetime annuity. However, a second option is an alternatively secured pension (ASP); more on this later.

If you die before age 75 while you are in income withdrawal, and haven't bought a lifetime annuity, you can leave your pension fund to your partner and any dependants. Their options are to:

- take some or all of the remaining fund as a lump sum which is taxable, currently at 35 per cent;
- use the remaining fund to buy a lifetime annuity;
- carry on withdrawing an income from the remaining fund.

This is just an overview of the options, so talk to a financial planner about all the options and how these options might work for you and your dependants.

Income withdrawal is usually not suitable for you if you:

- have a small pension fund;
- have no other assets or sources of retirement income;
- are not prepared to take a risk with your future pension income.

Income withdrawal certainly isn't for everyone. The following is a brief analysis of the advantages and disadvantages.

Advantages

- You are not locking into a lifetime annuity so do not have to make once and for all decisions about how you will take your pension income.
- Annuity rates might have improved by the time you come to buy a lifetime annuity, so you might secure a higher level of income than you would have done if you had bought a lifetime annuity at the outset.
- Your pension fund remains invested in a tax-advantaged environment.
- You don't have to take more income than you need.
- In the event of your death before age 75 you can leave the remaining pension fund to your dependants and they have choices about what to do with it.

Disadvantages

- There is no guarantee that annuity rates will improve; they might worsen and when you buy a lifetime annuity you could end up with a lower level of income than if you had bought a lifetime annuity at the outset.
- Income withdrawal does not give you the same security of income that a lifetime annuity gives you, and this may worry you. Your pension fund, and therefore the level of your future pension income, are dependent on the performance of the investments that your pension fund is invested in. If the income you take from your pension fund plus the charges is greater than the investment growth, it will reduce the value of your fund and consequently the future income you can take. To work well it is usually necessary to take a reasonable degree of risk with the investments in your pension fund, and you must be comfortable with this.
- You will have to review your invested pension fund and income withdrawals very regularly and this will take time and commitment from you even if you are working with a financial planner.
- Income withdrawal is not a cheap option; there are ongoing costs associated with it: financial planner's fees, investment charges, pension company charges. You need to identify all these charges and be confident that they are worth incurring.

What are short-term annuities?

Short-term annuities are sometimes referred to as flexible annuities or, rather mysteriously, 'the third way'. They are the area where insurance companies are showing how innovative they can be at providing ways for you to convert your pension fund into an income while staying within HMRC guidelines. While innovative and radical, some of the short-term annuity options available are both complex and expensive, so if the idea of short-term annuities appeals to you, do make sure you understand what you are buying and the potential cost.

Short-term annuities usually work by using a part of your pension fund to buy a fixed-term annuity lasting up to five years. Your options for this fixed-term annuity are pretty much in line with those for a basic lifetime annuity. In the meantime the remainder of the fund continues to be invested.

When the fixed-term annuity comes to an end you can buy another one or use the remaining fund to buy a lifetime annuity.

However, innovation is rife in this particular sector of the annuity market, so look out for alternatives that might suit you. But do be aware of what you are buying and the cost of buying it!

What's an alternatively secured pension (ASP)?

An alternatively secured pension works in a similar way to income withdrawal but has slightly different rules.

The government introduced alternatively secured pensions for a small group of people who had principled religious objections to buying an annuity. With an alternatively secured pension, rather than buying a lifetime annuity with your pension fund when you reach age 75 you can go on drawing an income beyond that age.

When you die, if you have any money left in your alternatively secured pension fund and you have dependants, then the money must be used to provide them with a pension income. If you have no dependants then the remaining fund can be donated to a charity free of tax.

The government appears to be concerned that alternatively secured pensions might be open to abuse and is keen to make sure that this does not happen. At the time of writing, the dust has not fully settled in this contentious area of pension legislation. The government may well withdraw this facility totally if it feels that abuse has occurred. So I suggest that you approach alternatively secured pensions with caution.

Summing up on how to take benefits from your pension plans

It is important to remember that when you come to convert your pension fund to pension income you are making important decisions that will affect the income you receive for the rest of your life. Do make sure that you are aware of all the implications of the income method, or methods, you choose. And I cannot stress this enough – even if you don't use a financial planner for anything else – consider using one for this part of your pension planning.

SUMMING UP

So, there you have it! As I said at the beginning, pension planning is a complex issue. The above is a simplified version of the bones of it and I do urge you to get professional advice. An excellent website to visit to find out more about pension planning is that of the Financial Services Authority, which I've already mentioned, at www.moneymadeclear.fsa.gov.uk.

If it doesn't do anything else, I do hope that this chapter encourages you to find out more about where you are with your current pension planning and helps you with any future pension planning.

USEFUL WEBSITES/CONTACTS ETC

To find out if you're contracted out of the Second State Pension scheme

Contracted-out helpline
Open 8am to 5pm Monday to Friday
You'll need your National Insurance number   Tel: 0845 9150 150

To get a forecast of your State pension

Retirement Pension Forecasting Team
Open 8am to 8pm Monday to Friday
And 9am to 1pm on Saturday   Tel: 0845 3000 168
Textphone: 0845-3000-169
Or access a forecast via the website
                                        www.thepensionservice.gov.uk
Or write to   State Pension Forecasting Team
                Future Pension Centre
                The Pensions Service
                Tyneview Park
                Whitley Road
                Newcastle Upon Tyne NE98 1BA

If you lost details of one or more pensions

Pension Tracing Service
Open 9am to 5pm Monday to Friday   Tel: 0845 6002 537
Textphone: 0845-3000-169
Pension tracing request form from   www.thepensionservice.gov.uk
Or write to   The Pension Tracing Service
                Tyneview Park
                Whitley Road
                Newcastle upon Tyne NE98 1BA

General

The Department for Works and Pensions
(can search for local office and obtain details of benefits)

www.dwp.gov.uk

The Pension Service (obtain free leaflets)

www.thepensionservice.gov.uk

Or telephone – open Monday to Friday 8am to 8pm

Tel: 0845 6060 265

Money Made Clear (the FSA independent website for advice and guidance on all money matters)

www.moneymadeclear.fsa.gov.uk

10

The Retirement Code: 87 things to do to make your retirement a success

'I think if our retirement is a success it'll not only be because we've carried on enjoying doing all sorts of things, but that we would be sitting here in 20 years' time still with a bundle of things we were wanting and hoping to do.'

James Dent

So what is the Retirement Code? What do you need to do to make your retirement a success? For each of us the answer will be different. Below is the wisdom distilled from the people I interviewed. Not all the points will apply to you but I hope that some of them do and that they will help you make your retirement the best it can be.

I hope by now you've realized that retirement planning is not just about financial management, it's about regret management, crossing off all the things you want to do in retirement. It's about probing deeper to try to identify the passions you may be setting aside until retirement, but which could well make a long retirement life worth living.

Michelle Stansfield feels that her retirement will have been a success if she has few regrets: 'I think there has to be a sort of contentment about "Well, I've got to 80 and I've actually done the things I've wanted to do," and there should be no burning ambitions left unfulfilled, no regrets. Regrets is probably a good word. If you could sit back and say: "Well, I've no regrets," I think that's as good a place as you can expect to be when you're 80.'

Our regrets in the short term are about action but our regrets in the long term are about inaction. Short-term action regrets got repaired because our minds tend to be resilient and we can recover from short-term mistakes. Long-term inaction regrets tend to stick with us and nag us.

One very powerful story told to me by a fellow planner involved a client whose wife had died shortly before retirement. The client confessed to the planner that before she died his wife had talked about the retirement future she would never have: 'She talked about all the things she wanted to do and never did and I'd never heard about those things before.' The planner told me: 'In some ways I think the lost dreams he never got a chance to help her achieve bothered him more than her death.' So... be brave enough to acknowledge your retirement dreams, share them and achieve them.

TIMING – WHEN IS THE RIGHT TIME TO RETIRE?

Some of the advice in this section of the conclusion might seem contradictory, continuing to work versus retiring, but hopefully it will challenge you to think about what would and wouldn't work for you.

There will never be a 'perfect' time to retire and you might have to make compromises, but it is important to identify what you really want to do with the rest of your life and take steps to achieve it.

So when is the right time to retire?

1. When you can afford to

Without doubt most people wanted to feel that they would be financially secure in retirement. As Sean Jeffries said: 'First and quite important was financial preparation just making sure that I could be reasonably confident that the money wasn't going to run out.'

The number one fear of virtually everyone I spoke to was running out of money in retirement. You won't have a great retirement just because you've made adequate financial provision. But having money gives you choices and might enable you to do more of the things that you'd like to do in retirement. Making financial provision for retirement might also mean that you can retire sooner rather than later. All the transitional and post-retirees I spoke to were glad that they had saved for their retirement.

Action point: Have you done the sums? Do you know how much you are likely to spend in retirement, including the potential cost of care in later old age? Do you know how much income and capital you are going to have in retirement? Constructing a lifelong cash flow planner which takes all expenditure and income into account might give you the confidence you need to say 'yes, I can afford to retire' – more on this in Chapter 5. Preferably do the calculations in plenty of time so that you have time to do something about increasing your retirement 'pot' if it is not going to be enough.

2. When you can both afford to retire

Richard and Samantha Jeffries discussed their retirement finances. Richard: 'I knew, because the mortgage was paid up, we could manage, and Samantha could manage on the widow's pension if I died first. We talked about this a lot and we'd done the sums and basically it was okay.'

Action point: Don't just do the sums, talk about it. For couples it's important to identify what the survivor will inherit in the way of assets and income; will it be enough for them to live on until they die?

3. When working life becomes too restrictive

If the nature of your employment isn't allowing you to do what you want to do outside of work, maybe the time has come to leave that employment and do something else. Maddy Lister left employment when she was told she couldn't have time off work to help out with her first grandchild: 'I was about to have my 60th birthday and could actually retire from my job which, although I enjoyed it, was stopping me from doing something else that I knew I would enjoy more.'

Action point: If your work doesn't allow you enough flexibility to do the things you want to do, what can you do to change it? If there's enough slack in the system to allow you to remain in your job, but with added flexibility around hours of work etc, then great. If not, and you can afford to, think about retiring. If full retirement doesn't appeal, think about moving to another job where there is more flexibility.

4. Are you putting off retirement because you're frightened of what will take the place of work?

When Michelle Stansfield was 53, her husband was diagnosed with cancer and died, and this changed everything: 'When Graham died I think, for me, the grieving was get my head down, get back into the job, because that's what I knew. So I think for a period of time I just forgot about retirement, just didn't even think about it.'

Action point: Consider why you are continuing to work; if it's because you enjoy what you're doing then great, if it's because you're frightened of the void that might come if you retire perhaps not so great. It might be worth considering some life coaching to help you plan your retirement so that there is an appealing life beyond work, something that makes you look forward to retirement. See Chapter 6 on life coaching.

5. When your work circumstances change

Michelle Stansfield eventually retired when she was 58, prompted by a change in the organization that she was working for. 'Things started changing in the organization, and that's when I stood back and thought to myself, do I really want to do this any more? Do I really want to get up at 6.00 every morning and do all of these things? There's got to be more to life than working.'

Action point: Adjusting to organizational changes may give you a buzz and might be just the thing you need to provide the impetus to go on working. Alternatively, as it did with Michelle, it may signal that the time is right to go.

6. When your health isn't robust

Gary Knight suffers from two chronic illnesses; neither is likely to shorten his life expectancy but both are expected to affect his mobility. Gary has decided that he wants to retire sooner rather than later so that he can enjoy an active retirement for as long as possible: 'I've decided, mainly because of my potential health problems and my loathing of commuting, that I would like to target 55 as my ideal retirement age.'

Action point: Retirement is best enjoyed when you are fit and healthy. If you know that your fitness is in doubt because of chronic illness, it might be worth seeing if you can retire early so that you can maximize the years of active and fit retirement.

7. When your partner retires and is available to play

Mary Edwards is considering how long she should continue working full time. She doesn't want to create more leisure time until Gerald, her husband, is available to share it with her: 'When I decide to cut back on my work is largely to do with what Gerald is planning to do. I'm preparing myself for Gerald to be more available for holidays and things at the end of next year. That's the time when he's thinking he might take time off for retirement so that's when I'll retire.'

Action point: If you are looking forward to doing more things together as a couple when you retire, it might make sense to try to align your retirement dates so that one of you isn't stuck at home counting the hours until the 'worker' gets home. This is especially true if both of you have worked full time.

8. When you're worried that you might go on beyond your 'sell-by date'

An eminent medical expert, Richard Jeffries decided to step down from his NHS consultancy work early: 'My work was incredibly responsible and – not actually stressful – but there was a lot of things depended on what I did, and I just felt there was a point where it was probably best not to hang on until the bitter end unless you had to.'

Action point: Be honest with yourself; if you are no longer able to do your job as well as it should be done, or as well as you would like to do it, stop doing it or consider moving on to something less demanding. Better to leave while you're at the top of your game than to be pushed out when you're sliding towards the bottom.

9. When you are sure you want to retire

While he 'retired' from his NHS consultancy role Richard Jeffries thought long and hard about retiring completely. He was 60 and the NHS normal retirement date was 65: 'On reflection I don't think that just retiring early for the sake of doing some amazing thing that you've not thought about is really very sensible, because what is five years? I mean, what are you going to do with the five years? Unless you've thought of that, then five years means nothing.' Richard went on to do other work within the health service and at 68 is still not fully retired. Richard isn't frightened of the void that might come when he eventually stops works; he simply enjoys his job and wants to keep on doing it.

Action point: Why retire if you are enjoying your work and don't yet have a plan for replacing your working life with a new retirement life? Don't just retire because you've reached a specific age or think it is the thing to do because that might lead to boredom. If you're worried about 'going past your sell-by date', explore the possibility of doing other work in the organization.

10. When you are really, really sure you want to retire

Just because things change, don't necessarily think: 'Right, time to retire.' Greg Eaton was 53 when he sold his business and 'retired' for the first time! 'And there I was at 53, without a job, suddenly thinking: "What can I do next?" I never thought: "I want to pack up." At 53 I was still interested in building.'

Action point: Think hard before deciding to retire; are you sure the time is right? Might you regret the decision in a few months' time? Retirement can be a one-way street; once you've left the workplace you are likely to lose skills and contacts so getting back in could be difficult.

11. When you have lost your enthusiasm

Greg Eaton enjoyed building his new business until in 2002 his wife, Jane, died. 'After Jane died there was the lack of enthusiasm to continue to build the business. Also, there were other things that I wanted to do.'

Action point: If you've lost enthusiasm for your work and there are other things that you would rather be doing, what's stopping you? If you have the opportunity to do things you have always wanted to do that will put zest back into your life but work is holding you back, see if retirement is a viable option.

12. When it's springtime

While the above covers the timing of retirement based on age and circumstances, the following refers to what time of year to retire. It was James Dent who came forward with this excellent point about timing retirement to coincide with spring: 'I was very glad that I retired in March because it's a time when it was all the outside stuff;

there's the garden, there's golf, there's travel. I think a lot of people retire at the end of the year. Unless they go away very smartly I think January and February could be quite a difficult adjustment period. I found it much easier to retire in the spring.'

Action point: We have already established that James, like many post-retirees, enjoys being outside looking in, rather than inside looking out. If you enjoy being outdoors, and you can influence these matters, it might be worth aligning your retirement with early spring.

HOW TO RETIRE – COLD TURKEY OR GRADUAL RETIREMENT?

13. The challenge of cold turkey

Deirdre Goode voices the concerns of many about the 'cold turkey' approach to retirement: 'Losing the responsibility associated with work. I think that's a huge weight off a lot of people, too much if lifted immediately. I think that what people dread is having a full-time job on, say, 1 December, and on 2 December having nothing. I think you've got to ease yourself into retirement and try and plan it before-hand and start doing things that you can continue with in retirement.'

Action point: Several post-retirees said that they had found it easier to adjust to their new life because they had retired gradually. Most people found that winding down from employment into retirement worked best because it enabled them to stay actively involved in some form of economic activity but gave them time to explore and develop interests outside work. So think about what you could do to arrange a gradual retirement.

14. Going part time

James Dent had a cold-turkey retirement, working full time one day and retired full time the next. On reflection he wishes that he had negotiated a part-time transition rather than an overnight one: 'Looking back, if there's one thing I would have done differently it is that I would have proposed to the company that I moved to two weeks a month. The guts of the job I could have done in two weeks each month and had I done that I think they would have jumped at it and I think that would have given me the transition I would have liked.'

Action point: Not everyone is in a position to negotiate a part-time transition with their employer or, indeed, arrange it if they are self-employed. But if you are in that fortunate position there is no harm in asking the question.

15. But be realistic, don't 'dabble'

The idea of doing your pre-retirement job on a part-time basis as a way of easing you into retirement may be an excellent one for you, but much will depend on the nature of your job and the amount of influence you have over your situation. Part-time may not work if you end up simply 'dabbling' in a complex area. Maggie Armstrong: 'There comes a time when you probably become dangerous, you work too little to keep in touch and you really should give up.'

Action point: Some occupations do not lend themselves to 'being dabbled in' on a part-time basis, so think long and hard before you decide to wind down by working part time in one of the professions. Will you end up dabbling and unable to keep pace with technological and legislative changes in your profession? If so, you might want to consider moving to something else which still uses your skills but in a less 'hands on' way.

16. Doing something different

It might be hard to arrange a gradual retirement by working part-time; much will depend on the nature of your job and the amenability of your employer. But while your own job may not lend itself to a gradual letting go, other jobs in the organization might. Of course this will depend on how you view the 'other jobs'. If you've been a department head you probably don't want to leave as the sweeper-up simply because that job allows you to retire on a gradual basis! Colin Matthews worked for a large company as a research scientist:

> I was very lucky. In the last two years with the organization I was put on secondment. I worked for a university, for the Prince's Youth Business Trust and I also gave talks on the company. When I retired from the organization, the university asked me to work two days per week. So I didn't feel that I was being thrown out of a professional job. I got quite a lot of variety towards the end and it was a gradual run-down. It was great.

Action point: While you may not be able to do your own job part-time, there may be opportunities to do other work in the organization on a part-time basis. Is there some project or alternative occupation that you could suggest that would be of mutual benefit to both you and your employer? Something that would enable you to gradually disengage from the company but would provide your employer with a benefit they may not otherwise be able to obtain from people external to the company? Maybe you could offer to spearhead a project, train people, give talks, arrange a secondment like Colin, or write a book.

17. Plan ahead

When Richard Jeffries was 62 he was offered the job of heading a research organization on a part-time basis and he jumped at the chance: 'I was thinking all the time what kind of transition I would need. And I never thought that I would simply have a cold turkey, you know, that I would simply shut the door and walk out. I always thought that I would want something which was a step down, so when the research thing came up I accepted it straight away because I realized that was exactly the kind of transition that was going to be ideal for me.'

Action point: Don't leave it to the last minute to think about the transition into retirement. Decide what you think will work best for you and plan it. Actively look for opportunities that will help with the transition.

18. Find out what's worked for others

Used to having his advice sought, Richard is good at asking for advice: 'I talked to a lot of my colleagues about this question of transition and about what they'd done and listened to the mistakes they thought they'd made. So I had given it some thought on the psychological level.'

Action point: Talk to colleagues and find out what has worked for them.

19. Gradual retirement for the self-employed

When you are running your own business it's not easy to arrange a gradual retirement. Julie Isles runs her own advertising and graphic design business. Until two years ago she was involved in the business very full time: 'I was working really hard and used to moan because I was working until two or three in the morning.' Julie didn't want to retire completely, partly because she couldn't afford to and partly because, at the age of 50, she still wanted to be involved in running her business. But she did become much more selective about the work she took on and now classes herself as working part time: 'My life has changed now I'm not working full time. I'm like a 13-year-old. I love doing endurance rides with my horse and I can do much more of that.' But the compromise that Julie had to make was a cut in income.

Action point: Julie had an income in the six-figure bracket when she was working full time and feeling 'worn out'. She has had to make financial sacrifices to give herself the freedom to do something that she has always wanted to do before she is too old to do it. If you are in the same situation, rather than retiring completely, consider how you might be able to give yourself more freedom to pursue other interests.

20. Having time to think about, plan and prepare for your retirement life – while you're still working

One great advantage of a gradual retirement is that it gives you time and opportunity to explore possible retirement activities while you're still working, but not everyone is able to arrange a gradual wind-down from their working life that gives them this opportunity. Your working life may not give you the space and time you need to plan ahead and you may have to accept that the early stages of retirement will be spent thinking about what you want to do rather than actually doing a great deal.

Belinda Crompton needed a thinking space between work and a fulfilling retirement life: 'I had no idea before I stopped work what I wanted to do, but I did know that until I stopped work I wouldn't have the opportunity to think what I might want to do because I was too busy thinking about work! So first of all I needed the space to allow what I wanted to emerge and to grow.'

Action point: Don't beat yourself up if you haven't had time to identify ambitions that you want to fulfil in retirement, or pastimes that you want to pursue, while you are still working. Accept that you might need to use the first year or two of your retirement to explore what you need to do to make your retirement life happy. Drift for a while, smell the roses and wait for inspiration to strike.

21. The two-year transitional period

Most transitional and post retirees agreed that you need a period of adjustment between your working life and your retirement life – a transitional period. And nearly all of them said that it can take up to two years to feel entirely comfortable with life in retirement. Joan Jarvis: 'My feeling is that I reckon it takes a good two years to find, I won't say find yourself, but find your focus and realize that you actually have a focus.'

Action point: Accept that it might take you up to two years to feel comfortable in your retirement life and you might find that, as Joan says: 'In that time you're going to fritter and waste time and maybe get depressed and not know what to do with yourself. And after that two years you realize there are things you can do and life does go on and there are people around, but it can be a very difficult two years.'

22. A transitional retiree going through the transition

Sean Jeffries, a transitional retiree, is currently going through the adjustment process between work and retirement, and while he is still involved in part-time consultancy work this is gradually diminishing. He made the excellent point that if you are busy during your working life you often don't know what you will find fulfilling in retirement because you simply haven't had time to explore the options:

> At the moment I am perfectly happy to drift. I don't know what my ambitions are but there might well be some that I will recognize when I come across them. Having time to stand and stare allows you to discover the things you actually want to do and didn't know you did at the outset. Here and now I haven't a clue what I want to do in five years'/ten years' time. But I daresay I'll encounter something and will enjoy doing it.

Action point: Well, here's one transitional retiree who certainly isn't getting depressed about his lack of focus, so don't assume that you will.

23. And bear this in mind – the need to 'show your hand'

If you are planning to retire before the 'normal retirement date' for your organization, or if your organization doesn't have a 'normal retirement date', you might be required to tell your work colleagues of your retirement plans well in advance so that they can plan accordingly. Nell Priest works for a professional practice:

I am required to tell my colleagues about my plans once I get to a certain stage. That made me realize that it's actually quite hard to do any serious planning when you're still working. I've got quite a demanding job and it's not easy to be selfish and say: 'Well, I need time out to think about the next phase of my life.' So far I haven't done anything at all about planning for my retirement, or even the transitional period into retirement.

Action point: If you are required to give advance warning of your retirement, make sure that you plan ahead so that you are well prepared and can ask the organization for any help you think they might be able to give you in the transitional phase.

WHAT WILL MAKE YOUR RETIREMENT A SUCCESS?

24. Building your ideal retirement life – before you retire

Your working life may be all-consuming and may give you no time to pursue possible post-retirement interests, but there is one constant in your planning – you. You know what interests you, what you enjoy doing, and that isn't going to change just because you've retired. Even if you are frantically busy, start to think about what retirement might be like for you. Think about the when and the how and what you might do in retirement.

    Action point: Think about it. Is there one thing that you are sure about, one thing that you know you want to do or one place that you know you want to be in, in retirement? Might that be a starting point for your retirement plan?

25. Watch what other people have done – and remember it's as much about what you don't want to do as what you do want to do

When Sean Jeffries was thinking about retirement he looked around: 'We started by observing what was happening to other people as they retired; and there are plenty of subjects for observation!'

    Action point: Observe! There are lots of examples out there to help you decide what you don't want to do as much as what you do want to do.

26. What motivates you?

Retirement doesn't change you as a person, as Richard Jeffries points out: 'We haven't stopped being the people we were. If you are motivated before you retire, you'll be motivated after you retire.' If you don't have a problem motivating yourself before retirement you shouldn't have a problem afterwards, but give it some thought.

Action point: Analyse what's important to you now and how important it will be to you in retirement and factor that into your planning. If it is to continue to acquire things, go on expensive holidays etc, it's worth making sure that you have factored that into your retirement sums.

27. Don't base your retirement plans on unexplored activities

If, like Michelle Stansfield, your work 'absolutely filled your life and everything else that happens, happens round the edges of the job', it is unlikely that you will have had time to develop hobbies and interests that you can carry on into retirement. You might be fortunate, your work pattern might give you enough spare time for hobbies, but it might not.

Action point: I am going to state the obvious here – don't base your happiness in retirement on pursuing a hobby or pastime that you haven't had an opportunity to try out – you might hate it. James Dent was convinced that he was going to become a sailor in retirement but: 'Before I went out and bought a boat I had an opportunity to do some blue water sailing. I helped crew a boat from Bermuda to Rhode Island for four or five days and I discovered that I didn't like it that much after all and Denise hated it.' So either accept that you are going to use the transitional period into retirement to explore various activities, some of which you may not find fulfilling, or make time to try them out during your working life.

28. And weekends might not be a good indicator of life in retirement

For Brad Isles, weekends are for relaxing, not for practising the activities he hopes to pursue in retirement: 'I don't do so much at the weekends, when I'm here, but I think that's because of the energy that I use during the week. I don't do weekend travel either at the moment because when I'm working it's just too tiring. But when I don't have to go to work every day, then I'm going to be much more willing to do other things, aren't I? It's common sense.'

Action point: For some people the weekend pursuit of hobbies and interests which can become retirement activities is part and parcel of their lives. Others, like Brad, see weekends as a time to relax and unwind from the rigours of their job. If this is you, accept that you may need to plan a transitional period in your retirement, possibly the two-year adjustment period referred to by post-retirees, to explore what you will find fulfilling in retirement.

29. Twenty-seven things to do in retirement

Two years before he retired, James Dent's firm sent him on a conference. One of his tasks was to write a list of 27 things he would like to do before he died. The list has formed the backbone of James's and his wife, Denise's, retirement planning: 'I told Denise about it and she did it. I refused to show her my list until she'd done hers. Then we showed our lists to each other. They don't have to be big things. For example, it could be to read a book that you've always wanted to read but never had the time.' Having the list helped them to focus on what they would both like to do in retirement. It also helped them to determine what they didn't want to do.

Action point: Think about drawing up a list of '27 things to do in retirement'. James's and Denise's lists were very similar and it gave them comfort to find that there was some commonality. On the other hand, there were individual things as well. As James pointed out: 'It's not a bad thing for couples to do but you've got to do your lists separately if you want that comfort – no conferring!'

30. There are no career counsellors for the over-55s

During your working life there is lots of advice available to help you make the best career and employment decisions. They usually ensure that you find a job that is both fulfilling and satisfying. But on leaving the workplace and retiring there is no advice available to help you determine what you need to do to achieve a fulfilling and satisfying retirement. This is where a life and business coach can help.

A life and business coach will work with you, helping you to define what you want to achieve in life and help you achieve it. It's not airy-fairy, it's objective, analytical and results orientated and it might be just the initial impetus you need to start planning your retirement.

Action point: Read Chapter 6 on life coaching.

31. Retiring might mean continuing to work

The government seems keen to persuade us all to work longer. The Chancellor has done his sums and knows that the State cannot support an ageing population unless we do all work longer. The government also knows that people who work longer stay fitter longer and are less of a drain on the NHS. If we are expected to work longer, that is even more reason to investigate ways of combining work with play.

If the definition of retirement is reaching financial independence then Barry Rudd retired before he was 50. However, he has continued to pursue a similar economic activity to the one he pursued when he was working for others but this time on his own terms: 'I think I will carry on doing some sort of economic activity and that will just go on until I am no longer able to do it. I don't think I'll stop at 55, 60, 65, 70 or whatever, because I find it interesting.'

Action point: Retirement might mean continuing to work, but on your own terms, doing things that interest you and that you've proved you are good at. Explore the possibility of becoming involved in activities or organizations that might offer an opportunity of work in retirement.

32. When your work is your play

You might be lucky and, like Sam and Joan Jarvis, your vocation might be your vacation and your work itself can be pursued as a pastime in retirement. Joan was adamant that this had helped her and Sam make a success of their retirement:

> Hobbies are very important when you are in your working life. I always felt that your working life should be a preparation for the time when you are not working. And if you haven't got a hobby you could be stuck. Sam had bird-watching, organ playing, books, natural history, a lot of things he did as his work was also a hobby. I always, always stitched from the age of about 12. I never sat down without something in my hands right through my life.

Action point: Few of us are in the fortunate position that Sam and Joan Jarvis are in, where our work is also our hobby. Indeed, several pre-retirees said one reason they were looking forward to leaving work and retiring was because they could stop doing what they were doing and never have to do it again! But if you are one of those lucky people whose work is also your play, think about how you want to accommodate work/play into your retirement plans. If you really enjoy your work, can you turn it into a retirement career?

33. Never retiring

Sometimes the transition into retirement can be so gradual, and your subsequent work in retirement so time consuming, that you don't actually feel as if you've retired. Certainly this is how Sam Jarvis feels: 'I know what you mean by retirement, and I don't feel I've retired, but I have changed my lifestyle. I am no longer working in television and making wildlife films but since then I've been really quite busy.' However, it's not been in quite the same way; contract work gradually gave way to freelance work that gradually gave way to presentations and lectures that gradually gave way to... all the other things that Sam is doing!

Action point: Sam and Joan's experiences should whet your appetite for exploring life beyond work. If it does, think about how you can create some space in your life on a gradual basis. Perhaps not retiring for several years, in fact doing it so gradually that you don't feel as if you have retired at all.

34. Changing careers

Joan Jarvis was pushed out of her designer job in television when her department was moved. She was in her early 50s: 'At the time I was working with another designer and we thought we would run an interior design company. So for a year I went on to a business development course and it was jolly useful, it taught me quite a lot about running a business.' The business never got off the ground but Joan found a City and Guilds course in creative embroidery and four years later: 'I was just walking on air. I had a whole new thing.' The course not only changed Joan's life, it provided her with a second career.

Action point: If you are thinking about setting up a business when you retire, it might be worth finding out if there is a business development course you could attend. But remember that when you are changing careers, in or approaching retirement, it may be that the first thing you try, or the second or the third, doesn't work out – they don't give you the fulfilment you are looking for in a second career. Keep on looking and, like Joan, you might end up 'walking on air'.

35. Joining forces

Richard and Samantha Jeffries are combining their skills and embarking on a new business making moving toys. Richard: 'We are thinking about working together with Samantha's design skills and my making skills.' Samantha: 'They are complementary skills so it's not that we're encroaching on each other's territory.' This is the first time they will have worked together on such a project. When I interviewed them they had just returned from a week's summer school learning about moving-toy mechanisms and designs: 'It will mostly, in the first place, be for birthday presents and Christmas presents and things like that because I think we need a lot more practice, but summer school was such fun!'

Action point: By combining your skills, can you and your partner, or a friend/colleague, do something together?

36. Finding new challenges

Several pre-retirees were anxious to identify and meet new challenges in retirement. Carl Armstrong: 'I would want to challenge who I am, not necessarily just for enjoyment but to discover something new.' Finding new challenges didn't appear to be a problem with any of the transitional or post-retirees, although most of them had been aware that it could be and had taken steps to do something about it. Richard Jeffries: 'I guess the key thing there, when you're approaching retirement, is to make sure you've thought it out and you've got something else that's coming at you that's just as challenging. So challenging that it worries you a bit whether you can do it or not.'

Action point: Do you have interests or an area of expertise outside your pre-retirement occupation that you could develop in retirement? If so, this might give you the 'something else that's coming at you that's just as challenging' that will help with the transitional period. Ernest Dennis deliberately does things that move him outside his comfort zone; he is constantly challenging himself. One of his challenges is to write and learn a new 'talk' and then deliver it at group gatherings. Public speaking is usually pretty high up on people's list of the most frightening things to do. So, what frightens you? If it's legal and not damaging to you or to others, it might be worth pursuing in retirement.

37. Keep on learning

To help her run her farm and wood on an ecological basis, Belinda Crompton started her retirement by doing two degrees: 'Since then I have been trying to put it into practice so therefore everything I do physically also has a mental base for me to think about and is part of a bigger picture.' The idea of going back to formal education, or even informal education, may not appeal to everyone but most post-retirees who were pursuing further learning seemed to be putting it into practical use.

Action point: Several pre-retirees said that they would like to pursue some form of further education in retirement. The combination of further education that can then be put to practical use, rather than education for education's sake, seems particularly potent.

38. Becoming involved in the local community

When you're working full time you might not have time to even get to know your neighbours very well. This happened to Joan Jarvis, so when she left work she formed a residents' association: 'It's gone from being a couple of parties a year to almost being like a parish council!' Joan was secretary for six years and as well as helping her to get to know her neighbours it's meant that she has become involved in local community projects.

Action point: Finding a way to give back to your local community benefits everyone, yourself probably most of all. But when you are busy working it's often hard to find space in your schedule to look for local projects, let alone become involved in them. But when you are approaching or in retirement it might be worth exploring what community-based projects would use your skills and that you would be happy to support.

39. Sometimes it's just not that easy to plan

Planning your retirement in advance means that you have to make certain assumptions about the future. But for some pre-retirees the future is so uncertain that it is not possible to plan. Gary and Gloria Knight have a disabled son, Thomas: 'Thomas's situation makes planning in advance difficult. Thomas finishes college in four years' time and we would like him to immediately embark upon some kind of independent life. The chances of that happening are, at best, 50/50. So, we're not making the complications with Thomas an excuse but they do make planning much more problematic.'

Action point: It pays to be realistic in your planning. Gary and Gloria have recognized that they will not be free agents in their retirement life but are endeavouring to work around it and plan the best retirement life they can.

And two final words of warning:

40. First word of warning – don't let retirement become a self-fulfilling prophecy

Whatever you do, don't let retirement become a self-fulfilling prophecy. Resist the temptation to say 'I've retired, now it's time for the slippers and the fireside' unless that is what you really want to do. I have been amazed at what people have achieved in retirement and the fulfilling lives they have led.

For the transitional retirees, those who have just entered retirement, the lure of just sitting and doing nothing is very tempting, but I suspect over time the novelty of that will wear off. The post-retirees who seem to be having the most fun are not watching too much television!

41. Second word of warning – don't make your retirement life as exhausting as your work life

However great the temptation, don't make the mistake of making your retirement activities as demanding and stressful as your working life, unless that's what gives you a buzz. Plan time out to do things simply for pleasure. It was Belinda Crompton who admitted that she was tempted to take on far too many projects and had to concentrate on slowing it down a bit. As she said, you don't get weekends in retirement, it's a seven-day-a-week job: 'It's only too easy not to allow yourself the time to do things simply for pleasure, the things that you might have done at weekends when you worked.'

HOW TO ENSURE YOUR RELATIONSHIP SURVIVES RETIREMENT

42. Period of adjustment

Without exception, all the transitional and post-retirees admitted that their relationships went through a 'period of adjustment' when they first retired. It stands to reason that if you have spent the last

40 years of your relationship working, each of you will have developed a life that does not accommodate, at least initially, being together 24 hours a day. Samantha Jeffries: 'I'd had the house to myself for 40 years and so my timetables have been turned over by just having someone else around. Not that Richard interferes or anything, but just having someone else in the house is a very strange thing to get used to.'

Action point: Accept that your relationship will go through a period of adjustment when you first retire and that this is completely normal.

43. Creating and/or preserving your own space and independence

If you and your partner have been used to having your own space and, to a degree, your own independence, you might want to work out ways of preserving this in retirement. Diane Dennis: 'Friends said to me: Keep doing what you've always done, don't let Ernest being at home change that.' Diane's determination to continue doing what she had always done worked well for her, as did deliberately planning that she, and her husband Ernest, would each pursue different pastimes and join different groups in retirement.

Action point: Work out a few ground rules to make sure that each of you preserves your independence. It might be that you decide to pursue different hobbies or interests at different times. Or you might have decided that what you are looking forward to most about being retired is being able to do more things together, as Joan Jarvis says: 'What's life about if you can't sit down and have a cup of coffee together?', although she did go on to say: 'But I think it's terribly important for all couples to have their own areas of interest.' Every relationship is different and the most important thing is that you acknowledge a potential problem, discuss it and agree on a course of action.

44. But don't reject your partner

If one of you has worked full time in a demanding job while the other has played more of a supporting role, it is likely that the supporting person has learnt to build a life of their own. Sarah Joyce: 'Well, there is a point that is often raised: "I married for better and for worse, but not for lunch". Often when you are married to someone who is very active and busy in their working life, you have to make your own life.'

So the question then is: will your lives gel when you come to retirement? Or have your lives become quite separate? Sarah: 'Will your partner feel rejected by you if you carry on with the life you made to fill in the gap while they were out working?'

Action point: Make sure that the person retiring is not going to feel doubly rejected – firstly by their workplace and secondly by their partner when they retire. Talk about the things you might do together in retirement as well as those things you want to do separately to preserve your independence and space.

45. Making allowances

Joan Jarvis had recognized that it might take some time for her and Sam to learn to live happily together on a full-time basis: 'I remember thinking to myself, it sounds awfully patronizing, "I'll give him two years" but that's what it felt like, and you've got to be absolutely patient for that two years.'

Action point: Accept that it might take time to settle down into retired life together and make allowances during that period of adjustment.

46. Keep each other in the picture

Used to going out of the door early in the morning, not coming back until the evening and having a full-time secretary to organize his day, Richard Jeffries found that it didn't come naturally to keep Samantha in the picture as to his daily comings and goings in retirement. Samantha: 'It would be very nice for me to know what's happening in the week because you just do make some allowances that someone else might be around, or want lunch, or perhaps do something together. If you don't know whether they're going to be in or not it makes it a bit difficult to organize, so I think a timetable will be very useful for both of us – a sort of family diary.'

Action point: Get a family diary, keep it up to date and look at it!

47. Gradual retirement works best

Most couples agreed that having a phased transition into retirement gave them more opportunities to gradually get used to being together on a full-time basis. Ernest Dennis had had a gradual retirement and when asked if this had helped her get used to having him around full-time, Denise said: 'Definitely, by the time Ernest was fully retired we were more or less used to each other's company. I was used to having him for lunch as well!'

Action point: Giving your partner and relationship the chance to adjust to spending more time in each other's space on a gradual basis is another good reason for considering a phased transition into retirement.

48. Working at a relationship is worth the effort

Most relationships do survive the changes that retirement brings. Indeed, several couples said that their relationships were stronger as a result of going through the process of adjusting to being together full-time in retirement. And the great advantage of being together in retirement is the companionship that being in a partnership brings. Nearly all the post-retirees who are on their own named coping with loneliness as their major challenge. As Greg Eaton says: 'I think a lot of what you do is better with two. Take gardening for example, I think it's much more fulfilling when you have someone to say "That's nice isn't it" and "Come and look at this" and "Cor! That's fabulous". But to say it to yourself – well, you just don't do it.'

Action point: So it's worth working at your relationship.

49. Talk about it – but things might not work out as planned

William Kennett began to realize that his relationship with his wife wouldn't survive retirement unless things changed, so they talked about it: 'We had several discussions about this and eventually, one day, my wife said to me the words "Well, I can't change" and the moment she said that I thought well, I'm not sure that I can go on living like this all day, seven days a week. I need something more.' The 'something more' that William wanted was the companionship he knew he would need in retirement and which he felt he didn't have with his wife. Shortly before he retired William and his wife separated, subsequently divorced and William remarried. He and Helen have been happily married for the past 17 years.

Action point: Be honest with yourself and your partner; if you are worried about how your relationship will cope with being together on a full-time basis, talk about it. It seems only fair to share concerns and worries so that each of you has an opportunity to address them. Now that people are living longer in retirement they are less likely to want to put up with a second-rate relationship in retirement. Not all relationships survive retirement, so if your relationship is important to you be prepared to put some spade-work in!

50. And if it doesn't work out – take heart from this story

Having planned and prepared for their retirement life well in advance, Belinda Crompton had no doubt that she and her husband, Derek, would have an exciting and fulfilling retirement. So it came as a total shock to her when, shortly before Derek was due to retire, he left Belinda for another woman whom he subsequently married. Devastated at the time, it took Belinda several years to come to terms with her forcibly changed retirement plans but now she admits it's the best thing that could have happened: 'Being by myself meant that I discovered different things and that's been my greatest satisfaction. But I didn't originally plan it that way and, at the time, I didn't think that way. But things changed so I changed with it.'

Action point: Retirement can act as a catalyst for change, as I suspect it did for Belinda and Derek – so beware. But if change is forced upon you, take heart from Belinda's story. What started out as something she had no wish for turned out to be a life-enhancing voyage of self-discovery and led to a far more fulfilling retirement than she had ever imagined she would have.

51. Make sure you're planning the same retirement life!

It is just as important to identify what you don't want to do in retirement as well as what you do want to do. It helps, of course, if both you and your partner agree on this issue. If not, some compromises might be necessary, but talk about it.

I was surprised when I carried out joint interviews with the pre-retirees that it sometimes came as a surprise to each of them what their partner thought they might like to do in retirement. It is healthy to have separate interests in retirement but it is also fun to do some things together and it's good to know what lines each of you is thinking along! Brad and Julie Isles have different ideas about what would constitute a happy retirement.

A talented artist, Julie would like to paint more: 'I want to do it every day so I get better. I want to improve. I want to go off hiking in the Australian bush and paint some pictures with my friend next year.

You know, just for a couple of years, but I know Brad would never want to do that. But I will do it.'

On the other hand, Brad wants to develop his interest in British naval history: 'I could happily spend a whole year touring, pottering round the coast of the British Isles. Doing a bit of sailing and some research and just exploring England, because there's so much that neither of us knows about England.'

Action point: So Brad will be exploring the coast of Britain while Julie is painting in the Australian outback. This is not a problem, indeed giving each other space to pursue separate interests going into retirement might be important in preserving a relationship at what can be a vulnerable time – but talk about it! To me it sounds exciting and means that each of them will have new and interesting news to bring back to the relationship. But make sure that you're both happy with the arrangements and make time for joint activities too. It might be a good idea to carry out the '27 things to do in retirement' exercise mentioned above to make sure that you are both planning the same retirement.

TWO OF THE HARDEST THINGS TO COME TO TERMS WITH IN RETIREMENT

Most of the fears about retirement, expressed by the pre-retirees, proved to be totally unfounded when I spoke to the post-retirees about them. But two fears appear to be justified: the fear of becoming irrelevant and the fear of losing social contact. So what can we learn from the post-retirees about coming to terms with these challenges?

The fear of becoming irrelevant

52. Feeling of usefulness

Often it isn't the status that people miss when they retire, it's the feeling of being useful, of being needed. James Dent had a high-status position within an international organization; he didn't miss the status when he retired but he did miss being involved at a strategic level in an exciting company: 'I miss the pressure; yes, I miss a lot of people coming up and asking things, wanting things and wanting to involve me. I miss that and I separate that out from a feeling of importance because I've seen an awful lot of people to whom these things are terribly important, but I honestly think they weren't for me. But I did like being involved and I liked being useful, and losing that left a bit of a hole sometimes.'

Action point: Give yourself permission to miss things; a chapter of your life has closed and if you enjoyed your work and working with your colleagues there are things you are bound to miss. But look around for opportunities to replace that feeling of usefulness in retirement.

53. Replacing the feeling of usefulness

James found that working for charities helped re-create that feeling of usefulness: 'I set out deliberately to get on the board of one or two charities to use my financial skills, and the idea was that this would give me some of the same sort of work, being on the board, doing things that I had always done for so long but it wouldn't be too onerous, too full time, and it's worked very well.'

Action point: If you think you will miss feeling useful, look around for an opportunity that might give you back that feeling of usefulness: charity work, non-executive directorships, community work.

54. Charity work/non-executive directorships/consultancy – you're much more attractive while you're still working!

It was during the last two years of working that James became involved with three local charities. He did this for two reasons: 'Firstly when you retire you start losing contacts, you're much more attractive when you're still actually working. Secondly, there's a hiatus if you leave it until you retire whilst you try to do this thing that, in principle, you want to do after retirement but haven't quite got around to.'

Action point: If charity work or indeed other work such as non-executive directorships, continuing consultancy work etc appeal to you then it could be worth exploring what opportunities there are, some time before you retire – while you're still attractive!

55. The potential downside of charity work

It was Barry Rudd who questioned how fulfilling charity work might be: 'Some of my friends have worked with charities and found it very frustrating. Coming from the world of business, they are used to working efficiently but find that other members of the charitable committee are there partly for social reasons rather than to get things done.' I asked James if he'd found working with charities frustrating; to a degree he has, but he's recognized that: 'As a non-executive director, whether it's a charity or a business, one is not in executive control. One has to work with people who are there and the culture that's there.' He did leave one charity he was working for because it was a bit chaotic but pointed out that there are lots of opportunities out there so there is bound to be one that suits you: 'I think the answer is if you're really unhappy you find something that suits you better. I've found once you start you get approached so you can move on.'

Action point: Working for charitable organizations has helped several post retirees find fulfilment and satisfaction in retirement, so it's well worth considering. As James points out: 'I've found that the charities I've worked with have been very business-like, it's not a bunch of amateurs' – but shop around.

56. Join the club!

Ernest Dennis gives a lot of time to the clubs he's a member of. One of the things that Ernest does for one club is to organize trips abroad: 'I think one of the big things is, when you join a club and you, say, become president or take on a job which requires a bit of work, a bit of organization, people appreciate it. And, you know, having appreciation from people is a big thing. It feels your life is worthwhile.'

Action point: Look around for something that will help you preserve that feeling of being needed and consequently appreciated. You might not be a club-type person but there are probably other efforts or organizations that could use your talents to the full and give you something back in return. RSVP, the retired and senior volunteer programme which encourages those aged 50+ to volunteer for projects in their local area, might appeal to you. Their website at www.csv-rsvp.org.uk is worth a visit.

57. Not becoming a waste of space

If you have been an expert in a specialist field, a professional used to having your opinion sought, retirement can be a difficult time because it is likely that you will go through a process of de-skilling. Richard Jeffries is still involved in various working parties and scientific councils so his advice is still sought, but he realizes that this will gradually diminish: 'The transition, intellectually, has not been difficult. I haven't felt that I've suddenly become a useless waste of space. The process of de-skilling I can sense is already beginning. As time goes by I will be less and less use to people. At the moment that's not bothering me greatly but I can see that it could become a bother because I'm used to being somebody whose opinion is worth having.'

Action point: If your job is very skilled and technical, think about how you might continue to use your knowledge and abilities after you retire so that you don't feel that you've suddenly become 'a waste of space'. But accept that over time the de-skilling process Richard refers to will kick in and you should look for a substitute to preserve your feeling of self-worth.

58. Don't become a 'ghost' or an 'albatross'

A cautionary word from Samantha Jeffries, who has observed the difficulties that some of Richard's colleagues have had in letting go of their work: 'There are a lot of people, with jobs as fulfilling and important as Richard's, who have nothing else in their lives. We both know people who, years after retirement, are still found wandering around the hospital looking for someone to talk to and somehow being around, when they don't have a job there, and that's really sad, they're like ghosts.'

Another aspect of this, pointed out by Nell Priest, is that the younger people in the organization you have left should be given a clear field: 'The other thing is after you've left an organization it's not very fair to hang around, like the albatross, round the neck of your remaining colleagues. Particularly for the younger generation who want to make their own mark, you need to leave them free to actually get out there and establish their own relationships with the client going forward for the longer term.'

Action point: Resolve not to become a 'ghost' or an 'albatross', a 'bar-propper-up' as Sam Jarvis called them. Don't return to your place of work after you've retired unless you are invited and can add something.

59. Tempo change

While sometimes onerous, as we have already discovered, having a full agenda gives a structure to your day. James Dent travelled a lot when he worked and his lifestyle was one of frenetic activity, so learning to adjust to a slower pace took time: 'Previously my agenda was not my own but it had all been there and it was a question of squeezing everything in. And whilst that working agenda can be bothersome, it does give a structure to your life and when you retire suddenly the time's empty. So there was a tempo adjustment that took a little while.'

Action point: Accept that the tempo of your life is likely to change, especially if, like James, retirement is not a gradual affair and one day you are working full time and the next day you are retired full-time. It might be worth planning some activities for the weeks immediately following retirement to allow your system to adjust gradually to the change in tempo.

60. Keep the diary going – helps replace the structure of work

Some of the transitional and post-retirees admitted that losing the structure that work had imposed on them had caused them difficulties in organizing their days in retirement. Richard Jeffries:

> When I worked my day was structured for me. I had a PA and a whole fleet of people who were running around doing things, organizing me. Now I'm not quite sure how to organize my day. There's lots of things I want to do and yet they're all rather disparate. Whereas before my day was rather homogenous; I went to work and there it was and I had all this stuff to get through and that's what I did. Now there's bits and I'm discovering that I need to impose some other kind of discipline on the organization of my time.

Action point: Practise managing your diary and work out a reminder system that works well for you. Several post-retirees admitted that when they first retired they missed meetings because they simply didn't look in their diaries!

The fear of losing social contact

61. Relationships in the workplace

By and large we are a gregarious bunch and nearly everyone talked about loss of, or the fear of losing, the stimulating relationships they had with work colleagues. The thing about work colleagues is that they are an eclectic bunch of people, perhaps people that you wouldn't choose to fraternize with socially. But this very mix is what can make work relationships stimulating. Helen Kennett was in her 30s when she married William: 'When we got together William was already retired and I was still working but I gave up work, and the thing I found, it wasn't giving up the work, it was not having the association with the people any more. I missed, to a certain extent, the people that I had worked with.'

   Action point: Think about ways in which you can continue to enjoy a strong social network in retirement. You may have many friends outside your work circle so this might not be a problem. Remember that your ex-work colleagues might still be working so may not be available to meet during the day. Indeed, maintaining work relationships once you retire could be difficult – depending on location, travel, their outside work commitments, etc.

62. Preserving the diversity

There is a tendency, when choosing friends, to choose people like us, with the same interests. But this doesn't add to the diversity which is so useful at bringing out different aspects of our own character and stimulating us socially and mentally. We don't choose our work colleagues and I wonder if one of the reasons so many transitional and post-retirees missed their work colleagues was because they missed the imposed diversity they provide. When she retired Belinda Crompton deliberately set out to preserve and add to the diversity in her different groups of friends: 'I'm a mix as well and diversity is the real spice of life. There are crossovers in the groups; I do have lots of sub-groups, shall we say, people who share several things.'

Action point: Belinda found it stimulating being involved in different groups of people with diverse interests because each group brought out different things in her. Might it be worth going outside your comfort zone and joining a club or organization that is totally new and different from anything you've done before?

63. Keeping fit socially

For Ernest Dennis, playing bowls wasn't just about keeping fit physically, it was about keeping fit socially: 'One of my retirement ambitions was to continue to mix with people. I mixed with a lot of different people when I worked and I wanted to do the same when I retired, so I took up a team sport that was healthy socially as well as physically.'

Action point: Taking up a group sport isn't necessarily going to replace the relationship that you have with your work colleagues, but it certainly helped Ernest.

64. Loss of being needed by your work colleagues

Sometimes it's not just the loss of social contact with work colleagues, it's the loss of being part of a productive team. In his last job as head of a research organization Richard Jeffries was responsible for a team of

116 people: 'I always enjoyed the company of all those people, their requirements meant my working day had a certain shape and structure, and it was instantly gratifying because, you know, you talk to people, you help solve problems and you go home in the evening and you think you've done a good job.'

Action point: Accept that you might miss the social contact with colleagues and the feeling of being useful to them. Sometimes just acknowledging the validity of a feeling is enough to help you cope with it. But also consider ways in which you could replace the social contact and feeling of usefulness: further employment, clubs or groups, charity work, work in the local community, teaching or mentoring, anything that provides you with an opportunity to work in a team.

65. Staying socially connected

It is staying socially connected, Ernest Dennis believes, that keeps him and his wife, Denise, mentally alert and able. When they left South Africa to come to the UK they left behind all their friends, relatives and colleagues. In an effort to get to know everyone in the street where they lived, Ernest became chairman of the residents' committee and got to know all 54 houses and their occupants. This active approach to socializing has stood them in good stead during their retirement. Ernest: 'Socializing helps to keep your brain active and also when you're mixing with people, holding conversations and such, it keeps you going.'

Action point: All you anti-social people are not necessarily going to want to follow this action point, but staying socially connected and involved with people was one thing that successful retirees said helped them to keep mentally astute. So... it might be worth getting out there and communicating.

66. And retirees are freer agents

And social relationships change as you get older, not necessarily just because you retire. Barry Rudd: 'We have some retired friends coming to stay next weekend. They'll be able to stay for a few days because they're now independent of their children. I've noticed that when children grow up, people do seem to start rebuilding their social relationships.' But Anita did go on to make the very good point: 'If you only have 30 days' holiday a year you are not going to spend too much of it going off to see somebody for 4 or 5 days. If you've got 365 days you can spread your friendship around a bit.'

Action point: So in retirement you'll have lots of opportunity to spread your friendship around.

TO MOVE OR NOT TO MOVE HOUSE IN RETIREMENT?

Opinions were divided on whether or not to move house in retirement. Previous generations' habit of 'retiring to the seaside' is being challenged. Nell Priest: 'To just give up an established lifestyle, which clearly must have suited you, to go and live somewhere else because people think that when you retire you shouldn't live in the city, for example, seems to me complete lunacy.' But things are changing. Nell again: 'I'm just slightly behind the first generation of liberated women and they are challenging a lot of these conceptions now as they are coming up to retirement. The idea that they should all go down and live in Bournemouth and spend all day knitting doesn't seem to appeal to them very much!' I'm glad to hear it.

67. Staying put

Several transitional and post-retirees thought the idea of moving house in retirement and risking losing contact with friends and relatives was sheer madness. Richard Jeffries: 'The big mistake I think for many people in retirement is to move physically to a point where their friends and family are so far away geographically that they've lost more than they've gained.' The Jeffries live in London and admitted they would make a move towards the centre of town rather than towards the seaside. Samantha: 'London is incredibly important. I couldn't live without the bookshops, art galleries, cinemas, theatres, museums, restaurants, shops, contacts, friends – and my family – they are terribly important to me.'

Action point: Think long and hard about moving house when you retire. Analyse what you really like about where you live now and whether a new location will enable you to maintain or enhance that.

68. Adapting your home to meet your retirement needs

Several transitional retirees had toyed with the idea of downsizing, moving to a smaller house that they thought would better reflect their retirement needs and budget. Sam and Joan Jarvis have lived in their house for many years. Initially, when Sam retired, they thought about moving. Joan: 'But then you think, where would you go? And it's pretty good here anyway. Where you live is even more important when you're not working because you spend more time actually at home.' So, instead of moving, Sam and Joan invested in their property to make it easier and cheaper to run. They've installed solar panels, cavity-wall insulation and automatic garage doors and intend to do more.

Action point: For Sam and Joan the answer, at least for the time being, is to modify their house to make it more cost effective to heat and easier to operate. If you are only considering moving because your current house isn't compatible with your retirement needs and budget, think about adapting the house to make it easier and cheaper to run.

69. And your housing needs in retirement might be more than you'd bargained for!

It was Sam who made the good point that modern-day retirees do have lots of interests and activities that mean their homes are not just the focal point of their living, they also become the focal point of their working too, so downsizing becomes a harder task. Sam: 'Actually the thought of moving is appalling, genuinely appalling. You should see my study – the stuff I've accumulated, not to mention the library.'

Action point: Don't assume that you'll need less room in retirement!

70. Moving to be near relatives

Moving near to relatives, whether it's to be near children or, indeed, near to elderly parents, is one reason post-retirees cited for moving. When they had been retired for several years, Ernest and Diane Dennis decided to move from Guildford to be near their daughter in the West Country. Diane positively looked forward to the move: 'We were ready for a change. We felt we'd been there, done that. We'd made lots of friends in the neighbourhood but their children had grown up and left home and many of them had moved away.' However, as always, Ernest was practical. They chose to move to the West Country, near their daughter Maggie Armstrong (also interviewed for the book), because she and Carl had just started their own professional practice and, as Ernest says: 'It wasn't likely that they were going to move around because it takes some time to establish a business.'

Action point: If you choose to move to be near children, accept that they might move away so it is important to move somewhere where you will be happy, even if the children do move. Ernest: 'You look for your ideal place. Of course, the kids might move away but that just makes it more important that you've made sure that you're retiring in the right place.'

71. If you move, be prepared to put some spade-work into your social life

One reason people are worried about moving house at, or in, retirement is the difficulty of making new friends in a new area. Diane and Ernest Dennis have been great 'joiners in' all their lives so when they moved they made a big effort to become involved in the local community via clubs, sporting activities and the church. Diane: 'When we moved we made lots of new friends. Well, we'd always been determined to join things. You can't make friends sitting back and expecting them to come to you.'

Action point: Many people felt that if they moved they would lose their valuable network of friends, although as Ernest and Diane found out, many of their friends moved away anyway. But accept that if you move you will have to put some effort into making a new social network.

72. Although sometimes you don't have to dig too hard!

When Barry Rudd retired he and Anita decided to leave London and return to their roots in the north. This was a very conscious decision. Barry: 'We always thought that we'd retire up here because we think it's a good part of the country.' Barry and Anita were fortunate that they had family close by, but did they find it hard to maintain their network of friends? Barry: 'No, it wasn't. Most of our friends live in the south but now they tend to come for a few days at a time so we've actually probably seen more of them since we moved here.'

Action point: Don't assume that moving house in retirement means that you have to lose touch with all your previous friends. Although the nature of your contact with those friends might change, brief outings giving way to longer periods of time spent together, so the friendships themselves might be improved.

73. Making sure you move to the right location

Moving house is disruptive and costly so it's good to get it right the first time. When they moved, the house that Ernest and Diane chose suited them perfectly but in retrospect they wish that they had spent a little more time researching the location. Ernest's advice to anyone moving would be to get involved in the actual area before deciding to move there: 'If you like bowls, see if you can go and have a game at the local bowling club. If the church is important, go to church and meet the people and see if you get on with them. If you're a member of a club, ask if you can attend a local meeting. We didn't do that and I wish we had.'

Action point: Obvious really – try out an area before you move there.

74. Second homes

Several transitional and post-retirees had holiday homes, either in the UK or abroad, and these formed the basis of both 'get away from it all' times or family 'get togethers'. Greg Eaton and his partner, Vicky Alder, have each kept their own houses and don't spend every day and night together. They have, however, bought a cottage together on the south coast and are busy furnishing it, it's 'their place'. Vicky: 'One of our ambitions is to spend good times there together – just the two of us.'

In spite of loving London so much, Richard and Samantha bought their second home in France as an impulse buy 20 years ago. They now use it as a gathering place for family and friends: 'When friends or family come over you see a lot of them. If we see them here, in London, we see them for dinner or to go to the theatre. But when they come to stay with us in the middle of nowhere we really get to know them.'

Action point: You will have your own views on holiday properties and properties abroad but, over the years, I have talked to many people who have had a second property that they use, very success-fully, not only to get away themselves but as a gathering point for family and friends away from the daily domestic arena.

75. The next big thing

Some of the older post-retirees are considering the 'next big thing', moving into sheltered accommodation or residential care. Often such a consideration is precipitated by an event such as a fall or no longer being able to drive. Maddy Lister's mother had to stop driving at the age of 87 because she had glaucoma: 'She had driven since she was 17 and that was almost like the beginning of the end for her and I dread that too.' So Maddy has decided not to move from the house she's lived in for the past 40 years. The house is a bungalow on the flat and near the shops: 'I continue to live here because it won't matter if I can't drive, it won't be that horrible cessation of life that people find difficult.'

Action point: Nobody wants to think about loss of independence but it will happen to most of us, so some forward planning when considering a house move later in retirement or indeed a decision to stay put might be sensible.

76. The next big thing – before it's too late

Always good at anticipating 'the next big thing', Wanda Purcell didn't wait until she couldn't cope with her old house – she moved in plenty of time: 'Where I live is very important to me. I lived in a big house and hadn't actually planned to sell up and move, but I met a person who was selling the perfect flat in the perfect place – old lady's flat – shops just a stroll along the level instead of climbing up a hill – ground floor flat, not stairs, and I bought it and moved here and it's been the most tremendous success.'

Action point: Don't leave it too late to plan a move into accommodation that is more suited to your physical needs. First of all, moving while you are still fully involved in the decision means that you acquire a place that you are happy with rather than one that you might feel is forced upon you. And secondly, you are still active and able to make connections in your new neighbourhood.

77. The next, next big thing

Many of us will end our days in sheltered housing or residential care homes. There is a real reluctance among retirees of any age to give this any thought or consideration. This is rather short-sighted in my opinion because, as with the action point above, making a decision about such an issue when you are still able to be actively involved in the process means that you are more likely to be living somewhere that you are happy with.

Action point: Read Chapter 4 on care in later old age.

KEEPING FIT IN RETIREMENT

78. Use it or lose it

'Uh – I do nothing during the week – no exercise. At the weekends we either do a walk one morning or afternoon, by which I mean three miles or so, more than that and we're both on the floor!' And this is Mary Edwards, our expert on ageing, who says that exercise is the one thing we can do to preserve both physical and mental fitness. It's obvious really, use it or lose it; you might discover a whole new level of fitness in retirement. And the fitter you are the longer you will be able to go on doing the things you want to do in retirement!

Action point: Read Chapter 3, 'Looking good, feeling great', a whole chapter devoted to staying fit and healthy in retirement.

FINANCIAL FITNESS

79. How much is enough?

'By the time I was in my mid-40s I began to be materially quite comfortably off in that the business was doing well and making reasonable amounts of money and I was starting to accumulate some money. And so, after a few years you begin to wonder about that and you think; is there enough to get by so I don't have to take this lip from my clients any more, or this lip from my business partners? What if? You start to ask yourself that question.' – Sean Jeffries

Action point: Preparing financially for retirement is essential and is what I've devoted several chapters of this book to. You'll find sections on financial planning, investing, releasing equity in your home and pensions. Please read them. And OK, you would expect this plug, but having a good financial planner is just as important in retirement, when you are using the assets you have acquired, as it is pre-retirement when you are building those assets. So... if you don't have a financial planner already, think about acquiring one.

BEING LONELY

80. Going it alone

For those transitional and post retirees who are alone in retirement the best and worst bits are opposite sides of the same coin. On the one hand there's the advantage of being able to please yourself but on the other there's the lack of companionship. Amy Pillinger: 'Being on your own allows you to be selfish and to please yourself. But then, at the same time, there's no one to discuss things with, or to knock on the window when you are gardening, and say "Do you want a cup of tea?" There's only you to do everything.'

Action point: There are advantages to being alone in retirement and being able to do exactly what you want to do when you want to do it. Focus on the plus side of being alone and able to please yourself. Michelle Stansfield, who has been on her own for five years: 'I've sort of got used to living on my own. If I want to slop around in my dressing gown I can do, and I don't have to worry if I'm not home at 9 o'clock, or whatever, so there are attractions to living on your own, which I never thought I would say.'

81. Don't let one become the loneliest number

Several single transitional and post-retirees said that it was not having someone to do things with that they missed. Even if you have a wide social network you could end up spending a lot of time on your own. How you feel about this depends on how happy you are with your own company. Deirdre Goode finds it hard: 'Although I have a lot of friends, I spend an awful lot of time on my own, particularly in the evenings in winter. I do go out to the theatre or the cinema once a week, but even so I'm still spending six evenings a week on my own with the curtains drawn. I've seen people get very old and be very, very lonely and I think as the years go on that increases.'

Action point: Easier said than done, but being proactive and making a positive effort to make sure that you only spend time on your own because you choose to do so might help to ease the loneliness. Wanda Purcell finds that keeping a busy diary has helped her: 'I look in the diary for the week ahead to see if there's a blank day and, if there is, I fill it with something. I do have a lot of friends. I ring them up. I plan my week so that something is happening every day. Not always necessarily seeing a friend but something is happening. I have something to do every day and I make a positive effort to plan that.'

82. Not becoming bitter and twisted

Retirement can be a lonely time, whether you're single or in a relationship, simply because you may not have the same amount of interaction with people that you had when you were working. And the problem can compound itself if you don't make a positive effort to stay socially connected. As a pre-retiree, Carl Armstrong, our Mr Misery, expressed concerns about this: 'I don't want to become bitter and twisted when I retire. I think the problem is that as you get older you tend to become more inward focusing. I think that the move there for me would always be to try to look outwards.' The danger of loneliness is that you can become very introspective.

Action point: Remain positive and be like William Hague's aunt who, when she was widowed, decided that she would never refuse an invitation. You may feel absolutely dreadful before you go out, but when you come back you feel a lot better. And people won't go on asking for ever!

COPING WITH LOSSES

Losses don't come with retirement, they come with growing older. As Michelle Stansfield says: 'My biggest worry about retirement is about getting old.' The potential penultimate loss is independence but you might have to cope with several losses before that; 'loss of independence by a thousand cuts'.

83. Loss of physical abilities

Several post-retirees talked about coming to terms with the disabilities that afflict us as we grow older. For Sam Jarvis it was the loss of hearing. Initially he was reluctant to do anything about it, refusing to acknowledge that it was happening. But eventually Sam acquired a decent hearing aid. Joan: 'It was when he couldn't hear chiff-chaffs, then he got proper hearing aids put in and he could hear bird song again.'

Action point: Don't go into denial – take remedial action! When he had a hip replacement in his 80s Ernest Dennis could no longer do breaststroke. He didn't even contemplate giving up swimming – he simply taught himself to do back-crawl instead. Attitude really is everything.

84. Loss of partner

The loss of a lifelong partner can be devastating, as Sarah Joyce, whose husband was murdered several years ago, says: 'The loss is enormous, and it's also the fact that you realize there is nobody in the world that cares about you – will ever care about you again – in the way that he did.'

For many couples this is the loss they really cannot contemplate, but the chances are that one of them is going to be left on their own. One of my clients confessed to me, shortly after her husband died, that she used to pray that she would die first because she didn't know how she would deal with their finances if she was left on her own.

Action point: Talk about it! Difficult as such discussions might be, they should enable you to focus on specific issues and come to sensible conclusions. Make sure that both of you are fully aware of the financial, legal and taxation issues surrounding your assets. Make a list of where all the important documents such as your wills, house deeds etc are stored. If one of you really feels that they couldn't cope with such matters on their own, appoint a financial planner that you both like and trust who would be on hand to give advice.

85. Loss of independence

The loss of independence is usually slow, a gradual chipping away at being able to function without help. Some of the older retirees are already coping with the first signs of independence erosion. Ernest and Diane Dennis were the oldest couple I interviewed. They were facing potential losses that younger retirees hadn't even thought about, such as no longer being able to drive; this would be a big blow to them. Ernest: 'Well, that's a very big thing not being able to drive, we're very dependent on a car.'

Action point: If you live near a bus route, near a train station and somewhere where taxis are readily available, being without your own transport will be less of an inconvenience. Such a consideration may seem unnecessary in the early stages of retirement but it is certainly something that Ernest and Diane are taking into account as they start to think about their next house move.

86. Turning a negative into a positive – and getting cheap travel insurance too

During their travels Ernest and Diane have had a taste of not being able to drive. Ernest again: 'We've travelled the world and before, when we got somewhere, we'd hire a car and drive all over. But then, of course, age stops you hiring cars. In certain countries you are not allowed to hire a car if you are over 80.' This age restriction has, to a degree, curtailed their travels.

Not to be outdone, Ernest and Diane looked for the positive side of their situation. Ernest now organizes group holidays for members of one of the clubs he's involved in, holidays where the transport at their destination is laid on for them. Another advantage of group holidays is that travel insurance, the bugbear of many retirees, is more easily obtainable for older travellers and cheaper too.

Action point: I find Ernest and Diane's positive approach to potential setbacks inspiring. They turned what could have been a life-inhibiting event into a life-enhancing one. You might have to accept that how you take holidays may have to change. The thought of holidays where transport is laid on, group holidays or cruises for example, may not appeal but they might become the only alternative to staying at home unless you can afford to hire a personal driver when you get to your destination.

87. Not becoming a stereotypical retiree

And for those who are worried that they might become a stereotypical retiree – I've discovered that there is no such thing. Each and every retirement is different and has the potential to be fulfilling to each and every retiree in the way that is unique to them.

Sean Jeffries:

> Firstly, I'd consider my retirement a success if I were still here in 30 years' time! Secondly, I think quite simply to have been happy in that time. If I've gone and done some interesting things then fine, but if I haven't and I've done that as a conscious decision, not because I was aimless, then that's fine. I don't give a toss about how anybody else judges my retirement, or them saying oh I wouldn't want to do that if I was retired – it's my retirement, I'll do what I want.

SO, REMEMBER – IT'S YOUR RETIREMENT!

The most exciting thing about retirement is that it provides you with an opportunity to explore and pursue all those things you never got a chance to do when you were working. But successful retirees agree that preparing for retirement, thinking about it and planning for it are likely to ensure that you have a more successful retirement than if you had just drifted into it. So I do hope that some of the '87 things to do to make your retirement a success' will help you to plan and prepare for the best retirement you can have.

Appendix: Useful contacts

CARE IN LATER OLD AGE

Better Caring	www.bettercaring.co.uk
Elderly Accommodation Counsel	www.eac.org.uk
Office of the Public Guardian	www.guardianship.gov.uk
Commission for Social Care Inspection	www.csci.org.uk
Age Concern	www.ace.org.uk
Department of Health	www.dh.gov.uk

FINANCIAL PLANNING

Financial Services Authority	www.fsa.gov.uk
Money Made Clear	www.moneymadeclear.fsa.gov.uk
Institute of Financial Planning	www.financialplanning.org.uk
The Personal Finance Society	www.thepfs.org

LIFE COACHING

The International Coach Federation	www.coachfederation.org
The Association for Coaching	www.associationforcoaching.com

INVESTING

Office of National Statistics (calculate your own, individual rate of inflation)   www.statistics.gov.uk
Money Facts   www.moneyfacts.co.uk
Money Made Clear   www.moneymadeclear.fsa.gov.uk

EQUITY RELEASE

Safe Home Income Plans   www.ship-ltd.org

PENSIONS

To find out if you're contracted out of the Second State Pension scheme

Contracted-out helpline
Open 8am to 5pm Monday to Friday
You'll need your National Insurance number   Tel: 0845 915 0150

To get a forecast of your State pension

Retirement Pension Forecasting Team
Open 8am to 8pm Monday to Friday
And 9am to 1pm on Saturday   Tel: 0845 3000 168
Textphone: 0845 3000 169
Or access a forecast via the website: www.thepensionservice.gov.uk
Or write to: State Pension Forecasting Team
                Future Pension Centre
                The Pensions Service
                Tyneview Park
                Whitley Road
                Newcastle Upon Tyne
                NE98 1BA

If you have lost details of one or more pensions

Pension Tracing Service
Open 9am to 5pm Monday to Friday   Tel: 0845 6002 537
Textphone: 0845 3000 169
Pension tracing request form from   www.thepensionservice.gov.uk
Or write to   The Pension Tracing Service
                 Tyneview Park
                 Whitley Road
                 Newcastle upon Tyne NE98 1BA

General

The Department for Works and Pensions (can search for local office
and obtain details of benefits)

                                         www.dwp.gov.uk

The Pension Service (obtain free leaflets)

                                         www.thepensionservice.gov.uk

Or telephone – open Monday to Friday 8am to 8pm

                                         Tel: 0845 6060 265

Money Made Clear   www.moneymadeclear.fsa.gov.uk

References

Barclays Capital (2008) 'Equity and Gilt Study', London
HSBC Insurance Holdings Limited (2006) 'The Future of Retirement: What the World Wants', London
Institute for Fiscal Studies (2004–5 Report) 'The English Longitudinal Study of Ageing', London
London School of Economics and University of Leicester (2004) Joseph Rowntree report 'Future Demand for Long-Term Care in the UK', London

FURTHER READING

Bernstein, W (2002) *The Four Pillars of Successful Investing: Lessons for building a winning portfolio*, McGraw-Hill, New York
Bogle, J C (2007) *The Little Book of Common Sense Investing*, Wiley, Hoboken, NJ
Ellis, C (1998) *Winning the Loser's Game: Timeless strategies for successful investing*, McGraw-Hill, New York
Hale, T (2006) *Smarter Investing: Simpler decisions for better results*, Financial Times Prentice Hall, Harlow, Essex
Malkiel, B G (2003) *A Random Walk down Wall Street*, W W Norton, New York

Index